A STRESS ANALYSIS OF A STRAPLESS EVENING GOWN

A STRESS ANALYSIS OF A STRAPLESS EVENING GOWN

Drawings by
Stanley Wyatt

Edited by

Robert A. Baker

And Other Essays For A Scientific Age

PRENTICE HALL PRESS

New York London Toronto Sydney Tokyo Singapore

Prentice Hall Press
15 Columbus Circle
New York, New York 10023

Published in 1987 by Prentice Hall Press
Originally published by Prentice-Hall, Inc.

Library of Congress Catalog Card Number: 63-16353
ISBN 0-13-852608-7

Manufactured in the United States of America

15 14 13 12 11 10

ACKNOWLEDGMENTS

Norman Applezweig, "Saga Of A New Hormone." Reprinted from *Drug and Cosmetic Industries* (April, 1955) with permission of the author and publisher.

Francis P. Chisholm, "The Chisholm Effect." Reprinted from *Motive,* with permission of the author and publisher.

J. B. Cadwallader-Cohen, W. S. Zysizck, & R. R. Donnelly, "The Chaostron." Reprinted from *Datamation,* Vol. 7, No. 10 (October 1961) with permission of the author and publisher.

Joel Cohen, "On The Nature Of Mathematical Proof." Reprinted from *The Worm-Runner's Digest,* Vol. III, No. 3 (December 1961) with permission of the author and publisher.

Dolton Edwards, "Meihem In Ce Klasrum." Reprinted from *Astounding Science Fiction,* Street and Smith Publications, Inc. (1946) with permission of the publisher.

S. Evershamen, "The Average Working Hours Of A Scientist During Lifetime." Reprinted from *The Journal of Irreproducible Results,* with permission of the author and publisher.

Frank Getlein, "A Report To The AMA." Copyright 1961. Reprinted from *A Modern Demonology,* Frank Getlein. Clarkson W. Potter, Inc., with permission of the author.

R. Arnold Le Win, "Logarithmic And Arythmic Expression Of A Physiological Function." Reprinted from *The Journal of Irreproducible Results,* Vol. 8, No. 1 (August 1959) with permission of the author and publisher.

John Masters, "The Abominable Snowman." Copyright 1959 by Bengal-Rockland, Inc. Reprinted from *Harper's* (January 1959) with permission.

James E. Miller, "How Newton Discovered The Law Of Gravitation." Copyright 1951 by the Society of Sigma Xi. Reprinted from *The American Scientist,* Vol. 39, No. 1 (1951) with permission of the author and publisher.

Horace Miner, "Body Ritual Among The Nacirema. "Reprinted from *The American Anthropologist,* Vol. 58, No. 3 (June 1956) with permission of the author and publisher.

Robert Nathan, "Digging The Weans." Reprinted from *The Weans.* New York: Alfred A. Knopf (1961) with permission of the publisher.

C. Northcote Parkinson, "Parkinson's Law In Medical Research." Reprinted from *The New Scientist,* 13, (January 25, 1962) pp. 193-195, with permission of the author and publisher.

R. W. Payne, "Peniwisle." Reprinted from *Journal of the AMA,* Vol. 172 (1960) with permission of author and publisher.

Nils Peterson, "Cosmic Sex And You." Reprinted by permission from *The Magazine of Fantasy and Science Fiction* (April 1961). Mercury Press, Inc. (1961)

Lester Del Rey, "Psalm." Copyright 1960 Great American Publications, Inc. Reprinted from *Fantastic Universe,* by permission of the author and the Scott Meredith Literary Agency, Inc.

J. Robertson & G. Osborne, "Postal System Input Buffer Device." Reprinted from *Datamation,* Vol. 6, No. 5 (Sept./Oct. 1960) with permission of the author and publisher.

S. A. Rudin, "A Psychoanalysis of U.S. Missile Failures." Reprinted from *The Journal Of Irreproducible Results,* Vol. 10,

No. 1 (August 1961) with permission of the author and publisher.

Rudolf B. Schmerl, "The Scientist As Seer." Copyright by the Society of Sigma Xi. Reprinted from *The American Scientist,* Vol. 47, No. 2 (June 1959) with permission of the author and publisher.

Michael B. Shimkin, "Principles Of Research Administration." Reprinted from *The Journal of Irreproducible Results,* Vol. 8, No. 2 (December 1959) with permission of the author and publisher.

Charles E. Siem, "A Stress Analysis Of A Strapless Evening Gown." Reprinted from *The Indicator* (Nov. 1956) with permission of the author and publisher.

Alan Simpson, "The Twenty-Third Psalm—Modern Style." Reprinted from *Washington University Magazine,* Washington University, St. Louis, with permission of the author and publisher.

Hugh Sinclair, "Hiawatha's Lipid." Reprinted with the permission of the author and the California Corporation for Biochemical Research.

Louis B. Salomon, "Univac To Univac." Reprinted from *Harper's Magazine* (1958) with permission of the author and publisher.

Leo Szilard, "Calling All Stars." Copyright © 1961 by Leo Szilard. From *The Voice Of The Dolphin,* five stories of political and social satire. Reprinted by permission of Simon and Schuster, Inc. (Paperback edition available at $1.00.)

Elmer W. Twente, "A New Tool." Reprinted from *The Worm-Runner's Digest,* Vol. III, No. 3 (December 1961) with permission of the author and publisher.

John Updike, "Cosmic Gall." Reprinted from *New Yorker Magazine, Inc.* (1960) with permission of the publisher.

Nicholas Vanserg, "Mathmanship." Copyright 1958 by The Society of Sigma Xi. Reprinted from *The American Scientist,*

Vol. 46, No. 3 (June 1958) with permission of the author and publisher.

F. E. Warburton, "Terns." Reprinted with permission, from *The Malpighii,* Newsletter of The Malpighian Society of Montreal. ——— "The Lab Coat as a Status Symbol." Reprinted from *Science* with permission of the publisher.

Warren Weaver, "Report Of The Special Committee." Copyright 1959 by The American Association For The Advancement Of Science. Reprinted from *Science,* Vol. 130 (November 20, 1959) with permission of the publisher.

Edwin B. Wilson, "The Bridge Of San Luis Rey." Reprinted from *The Journal of the American Statistical Association,* Vol. 25 (March 1930) with permission of the author and publisher.

INTRODUCTION

Is it unscientific to laugh?
—KATHERINE BRUNER

What's this? A collection of scientific humor, you say! But aren't the words *science* and *humor* mutually contradictory? The answer, of course, is a large "No" and this book is proof positive that science, like any human enterprise, does have its humorous aspects. Here you will find an amalgam of satiric science and scientific satire. Here you will find both scientists and satirists dedicated to the proposition that neither science nor man can hope to survive the rigors of our age without a sense of humor. For humor not only fosters perspective but it also provides us welcome relief from the soul-sapping monotony of our assembly-line labors, the ever-impending horror of thermonuclear war, and all the other aches and anxieties we find in our daily lives.

Since the scientists *are* human, you will find that their satire is also human and is as sharp and incisive as any being written. For the most part, these irreverences manage to avoid excessive bitterness in lampooning the fads and foibles of our day. Most of the selections are written in good humor and with good intentions. For those that are not, the arch-villain of the piece deserves all of the punishment meted out.

Although you may not know it, good satire is an exceedingly rare commodity. More than ever, the creation of the ridiculous is almost impossible because of the competition it receives from reality. In the old days, if the satirist was artful, he obtained his greatest effects by exaggerating the norm in such a way that the reader became aware of its abnormality. Today, the extreme is so commonplace there is little left for the satirist to do. As noted by Granville Hicks, "How in the world could anybody satirize a television commercial . . . ? What seems at one moment to be exaggeration for satirical purposes comes to look like sober description and the commonplace turns in the twinkling of an eye into the bizarre." In spite of this handicap, a great deal of excellent and enduring satire manages to come through. Some of the very best has recently appeared on the supposedly sober scene of science. I use the word supposedly because it is one of the explicit purposes of this volume to show that neither science nor the professional scientist is entirely sedate. Both the discipline and its devotees have their moments of intoxication.

Though many of the pompous would have us believe otherwise, as a group scientists have a fresh, sensitive and highly developed sense of humor. Unfortunately, the propagandists have too often chosen to emphasize the cold, inhuman and machine-like characteristics of the scientist. Rigor is made out as synonymous with rigor mortis and objectivity with obtuseness to the detriment of all. Especially to the young or the uninitiated, the image of the scientist is either that of an intense fanatic—careless of the feelings of others—who is willing to blow up the world if this is required to prove his theory correct. Or he is some kind of a nut whose behavior is eccentric and whose interests are far removed from practical affairs.

This is far from an exaggeration. As recently as 1957, a survey among high school students showed the scientist although perceived as a great man and essential to our way of life was also perceived as socially abnormal. The students saw him as one who talks incessantly about things no one understands, or as one who does not talk at all because he knows so many dangerous secrets he might accidentally betray himself. In the student view, he bosses his wife, neglects his family for his books and laboratory, and has no friends, or knows only other scientists. He has no social life and no other intellectual interests apart from science. He has a strange attitude toward money—either prostituting his skill and knowledge for a high salary and fame or he ignores it altogether, letting his family starve. He works at odd hours, and irregularly—only when the inspiration strikes him.

In certain rare instances, some aspects of this caricature are true. There are, indeed, weird people in science just as there are odd-balls in every profession. On the whole, however, scientists are remarkably normal and, like their blue or white collar counterparts, are creatures of their culture. They eat, sleep, work, make love, get drunk, marry, buy houses, pay their debts, have babies, drive automobiles, vote, swear, tell jokes, have toothaches, catch colds, buy clothes, read the newspapers,

play cards, own stock, carry out the garbage, make mistakes, and worry—just like ordinary human beings. And some of the scientists, like some of our citizens in other walks of life, often feel called upon to speak out against those things that rub them the wrong way. These are the ones that concern us here—the brave sons who not only speak out but do so with wit and wisdom.

Although the articles were chosen principally for their entertainment value, three other criteria governed their selection. First, those articles written from a future perspective, in which the author exposes some of the inanities of our age. Classical examples in this category are Robert Nathan's *Digging The Weans* and Dr. Szilard's *Calling All Stars.* Second, those articles in which masterful use is made of parody, i.e., wherein the author imitates the language of the topic under discussion for comic effect. No more delightful examples can be found than Dr. Miner's *Body Ritual Among The Nacirema, Hiawatha's Lipid* by Dr. Sinclair, and Joel Cohen's *On The Nature of Mathematical Proofs.* The third criterion for selection was articles exposing some of the pitfalls and frustrations that scientific flesh is heir to. For many competent, dedicated individuals participating directly in the joys and sorrows of research, all is not exactly well or wholly ennobling. There is a growing conviction within the professional body that neither the industrial, university, nor government laboratory is a completely desirable nor ideal working environment, for the highly motivated, creative, and problem-centered researcher. Nowadays, too much of the good scientist's life is a veritable rat-race of meaningless busy work and activity unrelated to research. He must supervise the letting of contracts, direct terms of assistants and play foreman to crews of technicians. Moreover, the distractions of numerous trips and committee meetings, briefings of important visitors, and public relations work—all of which are necessary to keep the whole frenetic business from falling apart—leave him in an intellectual daze. This situation is ignored by many, and even emphatically denied by some. Yet it is much too genuine for too many of our best scientific minds. The response to this situation in satiric form is typified by Dr. Miller's *How Newton Discovered The Law Of Gravitation,* Dr. Shimkin's *Principles Of Research Administration,* and some of Parkinson's newest laws—those prevailing in medical research.

There are, also, some deviations from the criteria since a few of the contributors are not by public avowal "professional scientists." Further, their contributions deal with the by-products of science—missiles, neutrinos, computers, mailboxes, and strapless evening gowns, for example—rather than the process of production. Yet, the surgical skill with which they employ the knife of satire is obviously the result of long years of training and study and is, in every sense of the word, "scientific." For present purposes, these contributors are duly and properly elected to membership in the tribe.

In summary, it is believed that all the contributors help us to better understand the nature of science and the men of science. Each of them has struck a blow against the "cult of scientism" and the "enemy" scientist who in the words of Norman Cousins ". . . makes his calling seem more mysterious than it is, and who allows this mystery to interfere with public participation in decisions involving science or the products of science." We must not forget that science is public property and we must never forget what Paul Weiss has called the *message* of science. In his words, "Science must neither let itself become dehumanized nor power-drunk. It has a mighty, not almighty, mission . . ."

In the search for truth—which is the mission of science—we must keep our sense of proportion and our sense of humor. God help us if the latter is ever lost. It is a curious thing that every attempt at the perfectly engineered society—be it an actual utopian community or a fictional distopia—has been characterized by its deadly seriousness. Perhaps the seriousness is the cause of failure. The lack of a sense of humor, the rigidity or unwillingness to bend is, perhaps, the basic flaw.

Thus, they shatter under stress. If an utterly humorless, deadly serious, maximally efficient utopia is in store for us, if this is what lies in our stars, we can only—as Dr. Schmerl notes in the final selection—be grateful that the stars are as far away as they are.

Whether or not this collection of protest will assist in the struggle for such understanding is a moot point. It is my conviction that it will, for as long as scientism rather than science, and as long as arrogant intellectualism rather than wisdom are permitted to rule, humanity will remain in bondage. Other than armed rebellion and speedy execution, satire—the acknowledged king of the comic arts—is by far the most effective means known for disposing of tyrants. Yet, even should the present rebellion meet with failure, the reader of the following selections will not only profit from the experience but will also learn that scientists, as a class, not only are human but have a remarkably fresh and ingenuous sense of humor. Today, thank God, it is still not unscientific to laugh!

Robert A. Baker
Fort Knox, Kentucky, 1963

CONTENTS

Francis P. Chisholm

THE CHISHOLM EFFECT
Basic Laws of Frustration, Mishap and Delay

Only one thing is certain—that is, nothing is certain. If this statement is true, it is also false.

—Ancient Paradox

Like almost all scientific discoveries, the general principles formulated here are based on the painful accumulation of data by generations of observers. To them I gratefully acknowledge my indebtedness for voluminous records concerning frustration and delays, a mountain of data which, until now, was without the firm logical theory necessary to relate it into a unified science.

Not that attempts have been infrequent to explain what happens when people try to get things done. The medievals considered Fortune a tricky goddess, and Shakespeare was close to the heart of the matter when he called fortune "outrageous." A diffused animistic explanation ("the general cussedness of things") can perhaps be traced back to primitive man. Burns missed the universality of the principle when he noted that plans "gang *aft* agley"; Conrad felt it when he noted that life combined "inexorable logic and futile purpose."

The clue to a strictly scientific explanation of the phenomena was discovered simultaneously by a number of mostly pseudonymous investigators reporting in early 1958 to that newsmagazine of the future, *Astounding Science Fiction.* In various engineering and laboratory contexts, they noted the constant appearance of the "Finagle factor" and of "Diddle's constant." No matter how carefully an experiment was set up, something *always* went wrong, usually in precisely the operation which *could not* go wrong. The difference between expected and achieved results could, in fact, be expressed in an exact relation, called the *Snafu equation,* involving the Finagle constants. An organization called "The International Society of Philosophic Engineers" published such observations as that "in any calculation, any error which can creep in will do so," and "any device requiring service or adjustment will be least accessible."

It remains only to generalize these and many other like observations from special fields into an underlying, perfectly general, unifying principle, operative in all situations involving human purpose. The generalization I designate as Chisholm's first law of Human Interaction, and state as follows:

If anything can go wrong, it will.

Further investigation shows that the logic governing the phenomena involved is non-Aristotelian, since a corollary of Chisholm's law may be stated thus:

If anything just can't go wrong, it will anyway.

All constructors of plans, projects and programs will note at once how these simple statements bring the order of explanation out of the chaos of their frustrations. In fact, the generalizations have that classic simplicity which we recognize in fundamental discoveries such as $E = mc^2$. Administrators, football coaches, generals and wives out to reform their husbands will all recognize at once the applications of the first law in their respective fields of endeavor. For example, the space planned for the key answer on any questionnaire form will always be inadequate; also, if you perceive that there are four possible ways in which a procedure can go wrong, and circumvent these, then a fifth way, unprepared for, will promptly develop.

In physical systems, it has long been recognized that entrophy, the measure of disorder, tends to increase and that highly energetic systems lose their energy to the less highly organized environment. A social analogue of this second law of thermodynamics may be perceived in the increasing disorder of a desk neatly organized at the beginning of the year. But contemporary attitudes are based upon the failure to realize

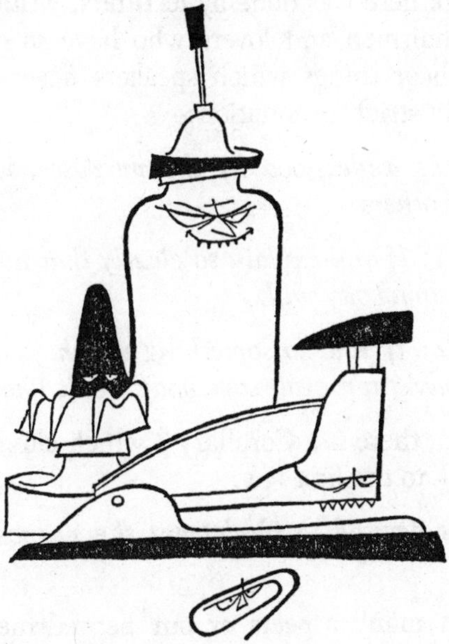

that this law of physics is also a social law operative in any human association. Hence, I restate it strictly in general form in Chisholm's second law of Human Interaction, as follows:

When things are going well, something will go wrong.

This law, too, has an obvious corollary:

When things just can't get any worse, they will.

I leave to the psychosomatic experts the reformulations necessary in their practice to help the ulcers of those who base their lives on an ignorance of this law. Their patient's situation is made the more serious by their inability to understand a second corollary which should be at once deduced:

Anytime things appear to be going better, you have overlooked something.

By tradition, these basic scientific laws have to go by threes, and hence I hasten to state Chisholm's third law. The preliminary work here was done by lecturers, writers, executives, committee chairmen and lovers who have so often observed that people hear things which speakers never said. To generalize, and in strict formulation:

Purposes, as understood by the purposer, will be judged otherwise by others.

Corollary 1: *If you explain so clearly that nobody can misunderstand, somebody will.*

Corollary 2: *If you do something which you are sure will meet everybody's approval, somebody won't like it.*

In addition, there is a Corollary 3 which closes the circle by referring back to the first law:

Procedures devised to implement the purpose won't quite work.

Implicit in many aspects of our benzedrine-and-sleeping-pill culture is the assumption that events codified by these laws are somebody's "fault" and should be responded to by anger, disappointment, Miltown or the increased production of adrenalin. Inclusion of Chisholm's laws as factors in the planning process should therefore reduce the degree of tension present and solve the national problem of adrenalin overproduction.

Horace Miner

BODY RITUAL AMONG THE NACIREMA

The very technology that makes our living simpler makes society more complex. The more efficient we get, the more specialized we become and the more dependent.

—THOMAS GRIFFITH
in *The Waist-High Culture*

THE anthropologist has become so familiar with the diversity of ways in which different peoples behave in similar situations that he is not apt to be surprised by even the most exotic customs. In fact, if all of the logically possible combinations of behavior have not been found somewhere in the world, he is apt to suspect that they must be present in some yet undescribed tribe. This point has, in fact, been expressed with respect to clan organization by Murdock (1949:71). In this light, the magical beliefs and practices of the Nacirema present such unusual aspects that it seems desirable to describe them as an example of the extremes to which human behavior can go.

Professor Linton first brought the ritual of the Nacirema to the attention of anthropologists twenty years ago (1936:326), but the culture of this people is still very poorly understood. They are a North American group living in the territory between the Canadian Cree, the Yaqui and Tarahumare of

Mexico, and the Carib and Arawak of the Antilles. Little is known of their origin, although tradition states that they came from the east. According to Nacirema mythology, their nation was originated by a culture hero, Notgnihsaw, who is otherwise known for two great feats of strength—the throwing of a piece of wampum across the river Pa-To-Mac and the chopping down of a cherry tree in which the Spirit of Truth resided.

Nacirema culture is characterized by a highly developed market economy which has evolved in a rich natural habitat. While much of the people's time is devoted to economic pursuits, a large part of the fruits of these labors and a considerable portion of the day are spent in ritual activity. The focus of this activity is the human body, the appearance and health of which loom as a dominant concern in the ethos of the people. While such a concern is certainly not unusual, its ceremonial aspects and associated philosophy are unique.

The fundamental belief underlying the whole system appears to be that the human body is ugly and that its natural tendency is to debility and disease. Incarcerated in such a body, man's only hope is to avert these characteristics through the use of the powerful influences of ritual and ceremony. Every household has one or more shrines devoted to this purpose. The more powerful individuals in the society have several shrines in their houses and, in fact, the opulence of a house is often referred to in terms of the number of such ritual centers it possesses. Most houses are of wattle and daub construction, but the shrine rooms of the more wealthy are walled with stone. Poorer families imitate the rich by applying pottery plaques to their shrine walls.

While each family has at least one such shrine, the rituals associated with it are not family ceremonies but are private and secret. The rites are normally only discussed with children, and then only during the period when they are being initiated into these mysteries. I was able, however, to establish sufficient rapport with the natives to examine these shrines and to have the rituals described to me.

The focal point of the shrine is a box or chest which is built into the wall. In this chest are kept the many charms and potions without which no native believes he could live. These preparations are secured from a variety of specialized practitioners. The most powerful of these are the medicine men, whose assistance must be rewarded with substantial gifts. However, the medicine men do not provide the curative potions for their clients, but decide what the ingredients should be and then write them down in an ancient and secret language. This writing is understood only by the medicine men and by the herbalists who, for another gift, provide the required charm.

The charm is not disposed of after it has served its purpose, but is placed in the charm-box of the household shrine. As these magical materials are specific for certain ills, and the real or imagined maladies of the people are many, the charm-box is usually full to overflowing. The magical packets are so numerous that people forget what their purposes were and fear to use them again. While the natives are very vague on this point, we can only assume that the idea in retaining all the old magical materials is that their presence in the charm-box, before which the body rituals are conducted, will in some way protect the worshipper.

Beneath the charm-box is a small font. Each day every member of the family, in succession, enters the shrine room, bows his head before the charm-box, mingles different sorts of holy water in the font, and proceeds with a brief rite of ablution. The holy waters are secured from the Water Temple of the community, where the priests conduct elaborate ceremonies to make the liquid ritually pure.

In the hierachy of magical practitioners, and below the medicine men in prestige, are specialists whose designation is best translated "holy-mouth-men." The Nacirema have an almost pathological horror and fascination with the mouth, the condition of which is believed to have a supernatural influence on all social relationships. Were it not for the rituals of the

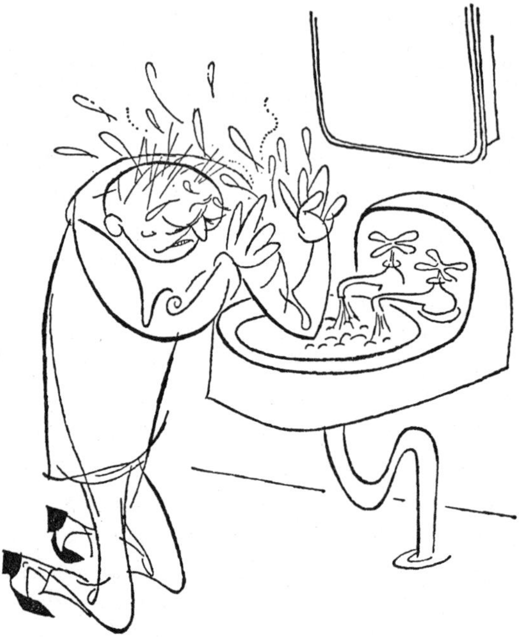

mouth, they believe that their teeth would fall out, their gums bleed, their jaws shrink, their friends desert them, and their lovers reject them. They also believe that a strong relationship exists between oral and moral characteristics. For example, there is a ritual ablution of the mouth for children which is supposed to improve their moral fiber.

The daily body ritual performed by everyone includes a mouth-rite. Despite the fact that these people are so punctilious about care of the mouth, this rite involves a practice which strikes the uninitiated stranger as revolting. It was reported to me that the ritual consists of inserting a small bundle of hog hairs into the mouth, along with certain magical powders, and then moving the bundles in a highly formalized series of gestures.

In addition to the private mouth-rite, the people seek out a holy-mouth-man once or twice a year. These practitioners have an impressive set of paraphernalia, consisting of a variety of augers, awls, probes, and prods. The use of these objects in the exorcism of the evils of the mouth involves almost unbelievable ritual torture of the client. The holy-mouth-man opens the client's mouth and, using the above-mentioned tools, enlarges any holes which decay may have created in the teeth. Magical materials are put into these holes. If there are no naturally occurring holes in the teeth, large sections of one or more teeth are gouged out so that the supernatural substance can be applied. In the client's view, the purpose of these ministrations is to arrest decay and to draw friends. The extremely sacred and traditional character of the rite is evident in the fact that the natives return to the holy-mouth-men year after year, despite the fact that their teeth continue to decay.

It is to be hoped that, when a thorough study of the Nacirema is made, there will be careful inquiry into the personality structure of these people. One has but to watch the gleam in the eye of a holy-mouth-man, as he jabs an awl into an exposed nerve, to suspect that a certain amount of sadism is involved. If this can be established, a very interesting pattern emerges, for most of the population shows definite masochistic tendencies. It was to these that Professor Linton referred in discussing a distinctive part of the daily body ritual which is performed only by men. This part of the rite involves scraping and lacerating the surface of the face with a sharp instrument. Special women's rites are performed only four times during each lunar month, but what they lack in frequency is made up in barbarity. As part of the ceremony, women bake their heads in small ovens for about an hour. The theoretically interesting point is that what seems to be a preponderantly masochistic people have developed sadistic specialists.

The medicine men have an imposing temple, or *latipso*, in every community of any size. The more elaborate ceremonies required to treat very sick patients can only be performed at this temple. These ceremonies involve not only the thaumaturge but a permanent group of vestal maidens who move sedately about the temple chambers in distinctive costume and headdress.

The *latipso* ceremonies are so harsh that it is phenomenal that a fair proportion of the really sick natives who enter the temple even recover. Small children, whose indoctrination is still incomplete, have been known to resist attempts to take them to the temple because "that is where you go to die." Despite this fact, sick adults are not only willing but eager to undergo the protracted ritual purification, if they can afford to do so. No matter how ill the supplicant or how grave the emergency, the guardians of many temples will not admit a client if he cannot give a rich gift to the custodian. Even after one has gained admission and survived the ceremonies, the guardians will not permit the neophyte to leave until he makes still another gift.

The supplicant entering the temple is first stripped of all his or her clothes. In everyday life, the Nacirema avoids exposure of his body and its natural functions. Bathing and excretory acts are performed only in the secrecy of the household shrine, where they are ritualized as part of the body-rites. Psychological shock results from the fact that body secrecy is suddenly lost upon entry into the *latipso*. A man, whose own wife has never seen him in an excretory act, suddenly finds himself naked and assisted by a vestal maiden while he performs his natural functions into a sacred vessel. This sort of ceremonial treatment is necessitated by the fact that the excreta are used by a diviner to ascertain the course and nature of the client's sickness. Female clients, on the other hand, find their naked bodies are subjected to the scrutiny, manipulation, and prodding of the medicine men.

Few supplicants in the temple are well enough to do anything but lie on their hard beds. The daily ceremonies, like the rites of the holy-mouth-men, involve discomfort and torture. With ritual precision, the vestals awaken their miserable charges each dawn and roll them about on their beds of pain while performing ablutions, in the formal movements of which the maidens are highly trained. At other times they insert magic wands in the supplicant's mouth or force him to eat substances which are supposed to be healing. From time to time the medicine men come to their clients and jab magically treated needles into their flesh. The fact that these temple ceremonies may not cure, and may even kill the neophyte, in no way decreases the people's faith in the medicine men.

There remains one other kind of practitioner, known as a *listener*. This witch doctor has the power to exorcise the devils that lodge in the heads of people who have been bewitched. The Nacirema believe that parents bewitch their own children. Mothers are particularly suspected of putting a curse on children while teaching them the secret body rituals. The countermagic of the witch doctor is unusual in its lack of ritual. The patient simply tells the "listener" all his troubles and fears, beginning with the earliest difficulties he can remember. The memory displayed by the Nacirema in these exorcism sessions is truly remarkable. It is not uncommon for the patient to bemoan the rejection he felt upon being weaned as a babe, and a few individuals even see their troubles going back to the traumatic effects of their own birth.

In conclusion, mention must be made of certain practices which have their base in native esthetics but which depend upon the pervasive aversion to the natural body and its functions. There are ritual fasts to make fat people thin and ceremonial feasts to make thin people fat. Still other rites are used to make women's breasts larger if they are small and smaller if they are large. General dissatisfaction with breast shape is symbolized in the fact that the ideal form is virtually outside the range of human variation. A few women afflicted with almost inhuman hypermammary development are so idolized that they make a handsome living by simply going from village to village and permitting the natives to stare at them for a fee.

Reference has already been made to the fact that excretory

functions are ritualized, routinized, and relegated to secrecy. Natural reproductive functions are similarly distorted. Intercourse is taboo as a topic and scheduled as an act. Efforts are made to avoid pregnancy by the use of magical materials or by limiting intercourse to certain phases of the moon. Conception is actually very infrequent. When pregnant, women dress so as to hide their condition. Parturition takes place in secret, without friends or relatives to assist, and the majority of women do not nurse their infants.

Our review of the ritual life of the Nacirema has certainly shown them to be a magic-ridden people. It is hard to understand how they have managed to exist so long under the burdens which they have imposed upon themselves. But even such exotic customs as these take on real meaning when they are viewed with the insight provided by Malinowski when he wrote (1948:70):

> *Looking from far and above, from our high places of safety in the developed civilization, it is easy to see all the crudity and irrelevance of magic. But without its power and guidance early man could not have mastered his practical difficulties as he has done, nor could man have advanced to the higher stages of civilization.*

REFERENCES CITED

Linton, Ralph
The Study of Man. New York: D. Appleton-Century Co., 1936.

Malinowski, Bronislaw
Magic, Science, and Religion. Glencoe, Ill.: The Free Press, 1948.

Murdock, George P.
Social Structure. New York: The Macmillan Co., 1949

Robertson Osborne, Joe & Gil

POSTAL SYSTEM INPUT BUFFER DEVICE

Anyone brave enough to challenge the idea that in a few years the replacement of man's brains will be the top industry of the nation is in danger of having his brains amongst the first to be replaced.

—Dr. Simon Ramo
Western Electronic News (March 1956)

Although no public announcement of the fact has been made, it is known that the United States Post Office Department for some time has been installing Postal System Input Buffer Devices as temporary information storage units on pseudo-randomly selected street corners. Several models are in use: some older ones are still to be found painted a color which may be described as yellow-greenish in hue, low saturation, and low in brilliance, but a significantly large proportion are now appearing in a red, white, and blue combination which seems to provide greater user satisfaction, although the associational-algebra value-functions remain obscure. Access to the majority of these devices is from the sidewalk, although a recent modification (including a 180-degree rotation about a vertical centerline) makes some of them accessible from an automobile, provided that the vehicle is equipped with either (a) a passenger in normal working condition, mounted upright on the front seat or (b) a driver having at least one arm on the right-hand side which is six feet long and double-jointed at the wrist and elbow. Figure 1 shows a typical sidewalk-access model Postal System Input Buffer Device.

OPERATION

Most normal adults without previous experience can be readily trained to operate the machine. Children and extremely short adults may find it necessary to obtain assistance from a passerby[1] in order to complete steps 4 (Feed Cycle) and 6 (Verification), or both. The machine is normally operated as described below.

1. *Position of Operator.* Locate the Control Console (see Figure 1). Stand in front of the machine so that the control console is facing you.[2]

2. *Initial Setup.* Grasp the Multi-Function Control Lever (Figure 1). This lever performs several functions, each being uniquely determined by that portion of the Operation Cycle during which it is activated. The lever may be grasped with either hand. With the other hand, position the input in preparation for step 4 (Feed Cycle).

3. *Start Operation.* Pull the Multi-Function Control Lever toward you until it is fully extended. It will travel in a downward arc, as it is attached to a mechanical But-gate hinged at the bottom. (The But-gate, so named because it allows but one operation at a time, is especially designed to make feedback extremely difficult.) Pulling the Multi-Function Control Lever at this time accomplishes an Input Buffer Reset and Drop-Chute Clear. These actions are of interest only to the technician, but are mentioned here in preparation for the following note.

[1] In this context, "passerby" may be defined as a member of the set of human beings having a maximized probability of occupying the event space.

[2] The Novice Operator Trainee may prefer to face the console.

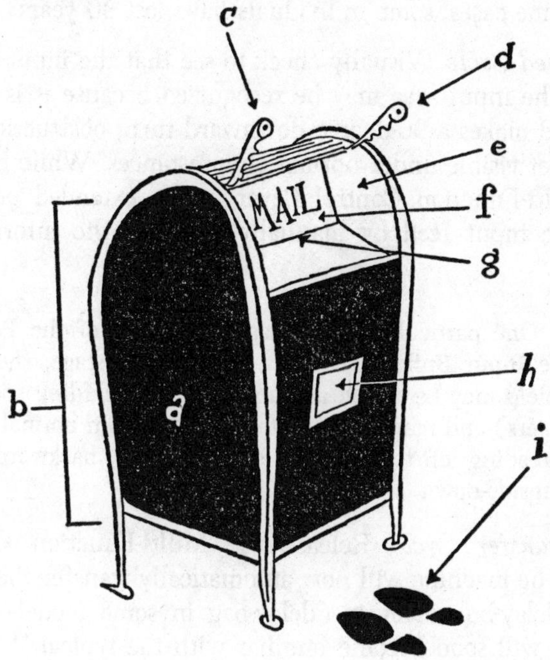

Figure 1.

a. Box or Bag Memory
b. Control Console
c. Malfunction Control Lever (Left Hand)
d. Malfunction Control Lever (Right Hand)
e. Input Area
f. But-Gate
g. But-Gate Hinge
h. Timing Chute
i. Initial Position of Operator

Note. The lever should move freely. If it does not, the memory is full and cannot accept further information until it has been unloaded. The operator may elect to (a) wait for a Postal System Field Engineer (a "mailman") or (b) find another Postal System Input Buffer Device. If choice (b) is elected, refer to description above; also see Figure 1.

Warning. Under no circumstances should the operator attempt to clear the unit; loss of a ring or wristwatch may result. In extreme cases, some individuals have lost 30 years.

4. *Feed Cycle.* Visually check to see that the input area is clear. The input area may be recognized because it is totally dark and makes a 90-degree downward turn; obstructions are hence not visible under normal circumstances. While holding the Multi-Function Control Lever in the extended position, start the input feed by manually inserting the information package.[3]

> *Note.* One particularly advantageous feature of the Postal Service Input Buffer Device is that, at this stage, the address field may be mixed alpha-numerics (including special characters) and may be presented to the unit in normal format (reading left-to-right and top-to-bottom), backward, or even upside-down.

5. *Transfer Cycle.* Release the Multi-Function Control Lever. The machine will now automatically transfer the input to the delay-box memory (delay-bag in some models). The operator will soon become familiar with the typical "Squeak" and "Clank" signals, provided on all models to indicate satisfactory operation of the But-gate. Actual transfer of the information,[4] however, is not signalled unless the information is very densely packed, in which case a "Thump" signal may occasionally be heard.

> *Note.* A "Bong" signal indicates that the information is unsuited to the Input Buffer Device and that a programming error has therefore occurred.

6. *Verification.* Pull the Multi-Function Control Lever again (see step 3), check to see that the Input Zone (Figure 1) is clear (see step 4), and release the lever. This completes one

[3] Perhaps better known to some readers as a "letter" or "postcard."
[4] *Op cit.*

full Operation Cycle. Additional cycles, when necessitated by large input quantities, may be initiated by returning to step 1 (above).

Note. Step 6 is not actually necessary for machine operation. The Postal Service Input Buffer Device has been designed to permit this step, however, to satisfy the requirements of the overwhelming Post-Mailing Peek Compulsion which affects most users of the unit and which has been linked by some writers to the "Unsatisfied Sex-Curiosity" Syndrome.

F.E. Warburton

TERNS

The turn of the century is certain to be made by a woman driver.

Attributed to
ALAN LADD

TERNS are a type of bird with webbed feet. They are, therefore, waterfowl, like ducks and penguins, and so may be found in the same books as albatrosses and eagles but probably not in the same books as wrens and wrobins. This is because waterbird watchers are so snobbish about dicky-birds.

Some terns are Arctic, some are Roseate, some are Black, and some are Caspian. In the tropics, some are Noddy, but nice. A few terns are Royal, but the majority are Common and proud of it—so proud of it that, in places, U-terns are prohibited.

Terns won't eat anything but fish, so it is no use putting out bits of suet and coconut for them in the winter; all you will get is dicky-birds, and you will have to buy a new book. Anyway, terns don't stick around in the winter. Arctic terns, for example, spend the summer at the North Pole. When it begins to get cold, they fly south to spend the winter at the South Pole, where it is summer. Having spent the winter at the South Pole, they fly North to avoid the winter, arriving at the North Pole in the summer while it is winter where they wintered. This remarkable migration, which involves flying more than 11,000 miles annually, was discovered when an Arctic tern, banded one summer in New Jersey, was found floating, belly up, in the Congo River some other summer.

Terns are found in pairs, if they are good, because one good

tern deserves another. They build their nests on the ground and places like that, and lay from zero to seven eggs. The usual number is zero, but many succeed in laying about two, or sometimes approximately three. The eggs are about the same size, shape, and colour as those of other birds. They get sat on for a while, and sooner or later some of them hatch. (This is but a brief summary of the combined findings of many ornithologists; space restrictions preclude a description of the life history of terns in all its fascinating detail.)

Baby terns just a few days old are the cutest, fluffiest little things. They will sit on your hand just as friendly as anything, going "chirp, chirp" and looking at you with their big bright eyes and vomiting half-digested dead fish all over your shirt.

Our knowledge of terns is growing every day, as more and more research on them is carried out under the auspices of organizations like the Defense Research Board and the National Cancer Society, but there is still much to be learned. We can be confident, however, that one by one the problems will be solved. Science will not rest while yet a single tern remains unstoned.

Edwin B. Wilson

THE BRIDGE OF SAN LUIS REY

If it would take a cannon ball 3⅓ seconds to travel four miles, and 3⅜ seconds to travel the next four, and 3⅝ to travel the next four, and if its rate of progress continued to diminish in the same ratio, how long would it take to go fifteen hundred million miles?

—ARITHMETICUS
Virginia, Nevada

I don't know.

—MARK TWAIN

(Reprinted from "Answers to Correspondents" in *Sketches Old and New* by permission of Harper and Brothers.)

MATHEMATICS may be either right or wrong. By this I mean that when you add 2 and 5 together you may get 7, which is right, or something else such as —3, which is wrong.

Or, to take a more complicated illustration, if you decide to fit some empirical formula or curve to a set of coordinate data, such as prices and times or populations and times, you may proceed in several ways. First, you may plot the variables and draw in the curve according to your esthetic sense. A curve so fitted cannot be either right or wrong, but only a matter of taste. There is no way in which the work can be checked. Of course, a dozen persons may be given the same sequence of points and be required each to fit the curve according to his taste. The results of those different fittings may then be compared to determine how much and in what way the solutions differ. I am not averse to this esthetic procedure. When the curve to be fitted is a straight line, it has been found by experiment that the solutions obtained do not, on the average, depart from the "least squares" solution by more than two or three times the probable error of the least squares solution, provided the drawing be made on an adequate scale. In cases where it is not important to check the work and where the precise least squares solution is unnecessary, the graphical method is often the best because it is the easiest to follow.

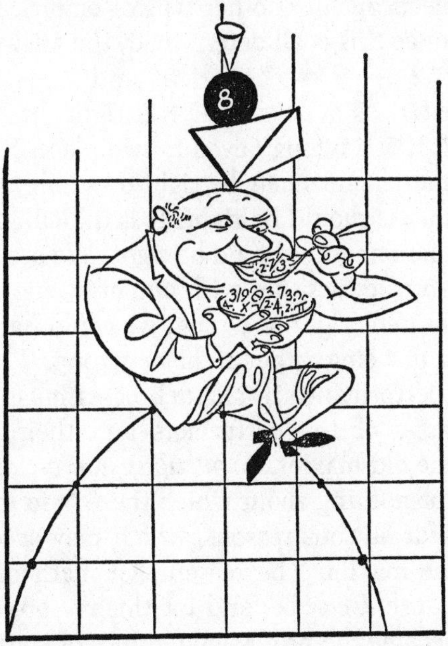

There are persons, however, who like to go through the work, or force their assistants through the work, of a least squares solution even when it is not necessary. And, of course, there are many cases in which to avoid the work of a least squares solution would be to shirk. One great advantage of such a solution is that it can be checked: it is either right or wrong. Every person who does the work correctly, starting with the same set of data, with the same weights assigned to each point and with the same empirical formula to fit, should get the same answer to that degree of arithmetic accuracy which is justified by the number of places carried in the calculation and without any regard to whether the original data justify carrying so many arithmetic places or not. It is a matter of taste whether one determines to apply least squares; it is also a matter of taste whether he assigns one set of weights or another to the various points, and it is often a matter of taste whether he selects one or another type of empirical formula to be fitted; but once this is all determined, the answer is right or wrong just as $2 + 5 = 7$ is right and $2 + 5 = -3$ is wrong—or better, as $\sqrt{2} = 1.414$ is right (to four places) and $\sqrt{2} = 1.305$ is wrong (even to two places).

Although mathematics may be right or wrong, I believe it is fair to claim that it should be right. It is difficult to undertake to prove that mathematics should be right. We are here dealing with a question of ethics, not with one of science. We do not expect an artist to be right or wrong; we could hardly accuse a metaphysician of being either right or wrong. The criteria of excellence of performance in all such cases must be based on tastes—the tastes of the performers and their critics, and, according to the old maxim, *de gustibus non est disputandum*, albeit I know of nothing about which there is so much dispute as tastes, and for obvious reasons, which may account for the necessity of the maxim. The reason that mathematics should be right is because it *can* be; and for this reason, to avoid disputes, it has become the professional ethics of those who apply mathematics to get that part of their work right. So widespread is this ethics that in practice one rarely tries to check the purely mathematical work of an investigator. It is not that the principle of corroboration which pertains to all scientific investigation is in abeyance, but merely that the mathematician is expected to check; i.e., to corroborate his own work so that the reader may take it on faith. Let us borrow the terminology of our societologists and say that it is in the folkways and mores of mathematicians that their mathematics should be right. Let us treat it as an axiom.

Why, then, should I make so much of the matter? Precisely because there are so many persons now using mathematics for the first generation in their respective sciences that it is advisable to set out what is the professional ethics of applied mathematicians. And because I regret to say that I have come across work by well-known investigators, in famous institutions, financed by generous foundations, work printed in journals of international repute, but unhappily so far from right that its wrongness can be recognized at a glance by any one really familiar with mathematical procedure. Evidently the work could not have been checked by the authors as it should have been or really read by an intelligent editor. This kind of writing and editing is a real imposition on the reader and necessitates some emphasis upon the duty of him who uses mathematics to get it right. Of course, we must not be too severe; accidents will happen and in any particular case it comes down to a matter of judgment as to whether negligence has been criminal.

Mathematics, assumed now to be right, may be appropriate or inappropriate to the problem in hand. This appropriateness is again very largely a matter of taste. One great advantage to the investigator of being familiar with a considerable variety of techniques and of the mathematical background of those techniques is that he has a greater experience and a sounder knowledge as a basis for his judgment as to appropriateness and he is, therefore, likely to have better taste in such matters. I made mention of the method of least squares. I wonder if many of you realize how pervasively that method penetrates our statistical procedures even when it does not appear on the surface. Suppose we add a column of figures and find the mean. Do we stop to think that the mean is the least squares solution of the problem of finding one item to represent the whole group? The mean is nearest to all the elements of the group only if we take as the criterion of nearness the squares of the eccentric departure and not the departure itself. It is the median which we should use, if our notion of nearness is to be founded on the departure instead of on its square, and I may recall to your mind that the great economist and statistician, F. Y. Edgworth, had a considerable partiality for medians—I know not why, perhaps merely as a matter of personal taste. Fortunately for many if not most problems, conclusions based on working with medians or with means are for practical purposes identical; but, when they differ, one may well hesitate.

To discuss this question of appropriateness of mathematics, let us take the purely hypothetical question, "Where should our association meet?" How might a scientific member from among us solve this problem? As to this I have no idea; the ways of scientists are often inscrutable. One type of mind would doubtless construct a spot map of our membership, scattered as it is about the country. If very conscientious, he would recall that many who are not our members but belong in associations which use statistics should perhaps be given some consideration, and he might therefore add to his spot map, with somewhat reduced weight, points to represent them. But how then select our meeting place? Should he determine the center of gravity of all the centers of gravity of all these points? Some would do so automatically. They would be, in fact, maintaining that the best point to meet would be that which minimizes the sum of the squares of the railroad fares that would be paid by all persons if all attended. And others might reason that what we needed was the point of greatest concentration of our population on the ground that it would be of maximum convenience to the greatest number—a just procedure, provided not many would come from a distance anyhow. This would be selecting the mode. Still others might feel that all interests were best met by that point which would make the sum of the railroad fares least, being in that median sense the point nearest to the whole membership and, thus, presumably most convenient on the whole. It is clear that the scientific solution could be obtained only after determining that type of mathematical formulation which was most appropriate to the problem, and this determination would be a matter of taste.

Fortunately, we all know that we may be spared such a scientific determination of the place where we shall meet. Like as not, nobody would be satisfied with the solution anyway and at all events there would be years of dispute over the appropriateness of any methodology. Much more practical means suffice. The Economic Association determines willy-nilly to come to Washington; the Political Scientists feel an irresistible urge to celebrate their twenty-fifth anniversary at New Orleans and the rest of us decide where we will go only after much discussion and perchance with small rational basis. This is one of those cases where pretty much all mathematics is inappropriate, where any mathematics whatsoever will give an entirely false sense of precision to a problem in which no precision inheres. And there are many problems in economics or sociology or the public health which are as yet very much in the same position and where we need not so much some kind of mathematics or some particular statistical technique as a general survey of a wide range of facts, many of them qualitative, which may serve as a basis for some decision.

Probably the majority of problems to which the statistician must turn his attention are in reality somewhat intermediate between those in which the technique to be applied is clear and those in which no technique, at least of a mathematical sort, is advisable. In this methodological no-man's-land, the statistician must do the best he can. He may have to develop a new technique; in that case he has two chief reliances: first and foremost, a sound and wide acquaintance with the field of activity in which he has to operate; and second, a good mathematical background, because it is from that that all techniques are developed. But if choice must be made between familiarity with his subject and familiarity with mathematics, I should unhesitatingly prefer the former. Mathematics is a queer horse and all too easily runs away with its rider; and then there is such a satisfaction in trying its various gaits in all sorts of roads that many a rider has gone off in almost the opposite direction from the path he should have followed in his pursuit of the solution to some scientific problem; he may have ridden right over his solution to some purely fantastic goal.

Each person has to do the best he can to bring to bear upon his work the talents and the training that he has. If I may be pardoned a personal confession, I will say that I have never been sorry that in my youth I acquired an unusually good acquaintance with mathematics. At times, when engaged upon some statistical problem in physics, I have needed to learn new mathematics, but for the most part my early training has sufficed not only to let me follow the mathematics of others, but, so to speak, to see through it with an assurance which sometimes convinced me that it was hollow. And if in my present studies I use but little of the vast amount I have once learned, it is not because I do not like the exercise of using it but because I prefer tools more appropriate to my job, even though not so refined—one gets ahead faster.

Mathematics may be right or wrong, it may be appropriate or inappropriate, it may be useful or useless. There is many a useless problem. Sometimes one cannot see it is useless until much time has been spent upon it. But consider this: I have a field in New Hampshire much covered with stones, rocks and boulders. With sufficient energy I could weigh all those objects, divide the weights into suitable intervals, plot a histogram and fit a frequency function. That would be scientific observation followed by mathematical treatment of the observations. The problem is obviously statistical. It would keep me occupied for some time. But what would be the use? Of course, if I knew enough about geology to be confident that my field was a fair sample of a large group of fields and if there was any geological or agricultural or constructional or other interest to be served in determining a frequency function of the weight of superficial stones from small to large from a "sample" field, the job might not be useless but useful. But there seems at present no good purpose to be served by its doing. And often I wonder in some of my reading whether the hard work the author has done, though correct and appropriate in its mathematics, may not be quite useless.

What we need to foster is useful, appropriate, correct mathematics applied to worthwhile, scientific problems, and worthwhile scientific problems whether or not they have reached the stage where any considerable use of mathematics is helpful. And in these vital matters, we have far more need of good taste and a sure instinct than is commonly believed, for it is so often only in the future that we can get a statistical estimate of the worthwhileness of present activities. Happy is the statistical investigator who can use all his techniques with discretion, and happy the teacher who can give his students some sense of proportion as well as a group of methods in such a conglomerate field as statistics.

Placed as I was upon the program between sociology and economics, represented by such giants as Presidents Ogburn and Gay, the one interested in making himself a mental centrifuge to precipitate the facts of recent social change from that murky colloidal solution we call the present, the other bent on crystallizing out from the subcooled liquor of our past the solid course of prices, it was quite impossible for me to determine whether I was to be the meat of your sandwich or the comic relief of your tragedy. Without pausing now to suggest an answer to this question, but rather in the continuing line of my previous remarks, may I direct your attention to that interesting statistical treatise *The Bridge of San Luis Rey*, by Thornton Wilder. Some of you recall the story. The bridge fell, killing five persons, and the devout Brother Juniper was struck by the question: Why did this happen to those five? And determined to surmise the reason of their taking off. It seemed to him that it was high time for theology to take its place among the exact sciences and he had long intended putting it there. What he had lacked was an opportunity for observation under *proper control.* Previous happenings had been involved, but here was a sheer Act of God and at last His intentions could be studied in a pure state. It was not, however, Brother Juniper's first essay in scientifically examining the ways of God to man. There had been a deadly pestilence of smallpox in his village and he had recently drawn up a diagram of the characteristics of fifteen victims and fifteen survivors, the statistics of their value *sub specie aeternitatis.* Each soul was rated upon a basis of ten as regards its goodness, its piety and its usefulness to its family group as follows:

	Goodness	*Piety*	*Usefulness*
Alfonso G.	4	4	10
Nina	2	5	10
Manuel B.	10	10	0
Alfonso V.	−8	−10	10
Vera N.	0	10	10

The investigation developed difficulties: almost every soul in this little community turned out to be economically indispensable, and the column headed "Usefulness" was all but useless; negative signs had to be introduced to distinguish from the good and bad those who were not only bad (Grade O) in and of themselves but actively led others into wickedness. From all this data the good scientific friar contrived an index for each person. He added up the total for the victims and compared it with the total for survivors—to discover that the dead were five times more worth saving. And then, taking a walk by the Pacific, he tore up his findings and cast them into the ocean—a most profitable mode of publication and in a medium of the widest circulation.

So when he came to study his one great chance, the collapse of the bridge with its five victims, having experienced the bitter disappointments of statistical procedure, Brother Juniper forsook the method of W. F. Ogburn for that of W. I. Thomas—the case study. In compiling his book on these five victims, he omitted no slightest detail for fear he might lose some guiding hint. He put everything down in the hope that the countless facts would suddenly start to move, to assemble and to betray their secret. Of one, the Marquesa de Montemayor, he learned from her cook that she had lived almost entirely on rice, fish and a little fruit, and he put it down on the chance that it would some day reveal a spiritual trait to aid in sifting the inscrutable ways of God. From another, he learned that she had come unbidden to his receptions to steal the spoons. A book-seller testified that she had been one of the three most cultivated persons in town. The midwife declared that she had called upon her with morbid questions until she became a nuisance; a servant that though absent-minded she had been a compact of goodness. And so with many another in her respect and in that of the other four. We may pass over the conclusions to state that the book, being finished, was pronounced heretical and our scientific theologist Brother Juniper was burned alive with it—apparently to the great regret of everybody, but the simple persons of his time may not have had our overburdening experience with questionnairing.

With an apology to you and to Mr. Wilder for these few free quotations from *The Bridge of San Luis Rey* couched in a crude English that does him no justice, I will leave you with the suggestion that you study further this remarkable statistical romance, and I will venture the hope that should the author make a few dollars extra from royalties because of this hint of mine, he should apply them to securing a membership in our statistical association. Some of us need him in our business.

John Updike

COSMIC GALL

Every second, hundreds of billions of these neutrinos pass through each square inch of our bodies coming from above during the day and from below at night, when the sun is shining on the other side of the earth!

—M. A. RUDERMAN

NEUTRINOS, they are very small.
They have no charge and have no mass
And do not interact at all.
The earth is just a silly ball
To them, through which they simply pass,
Like dustmaids down a drafty hall
Or photons through a sheet of glass.
They snub the most exquisite gas,
Ignore the most substantial wall,
Cold-shoulder steel and sounding brass,
Insult the stallion in his stall,
And scorning barriers of class,
Infiltrate you and me! Like tall
And painless guillotines, they fall
Down through our heads into the grass.

At night, they enter at Nepal
And pierce the lover and his lass
From underneath the bed—you call
It wonderful; I call it crass.

John Masters

THE ABOMINABLE SNOWMAN

Thomas Henry Huxley, in 1860, debated the cause of evolution with Bishop Wilberforce. The good Bishop concluded his attack on evolution by asking Huxley whether his descent from the ape was on his father's or his mother's side.

Huxley's reply was as follows:

If then the question is put to me would I rather have a miserable ape for a grandfather or a man highly endowed by nature and possessing great means and influence and yet who employs those faculties and that influence for the mere purpose of introducing ridicule into a grave scientific discussion—I unhesitatingly affirm my preference for the ape.

ARMCHAIR scientists can sneer all they like, but a former British Army officer, who prowled around the Himalayas for years, insists that Something Is Up There. Two Somethings, in fact, both of them quite dreadful . . . .

The case of the Abominable Snowman, or Yeti, was first drawn to my attention twenty years ago by H. W. Tilman. Tilman had led an unsuccessful attempt on Everest and at the end of his official account, *Mount Everest, 1938*, he added a certain Appendix B, subtitled "Anthropology or Zoology with Particular Reference to the 'Abominable Snowman.' " Tilman can be a funny writer, and he is one of the few high-altitude men who allow the upper lip to tremble in the face of comic or disastrous incidents; but he does have a tendency to flippancy, even facetiousness, and the passing references in his appendix to *Homo Niveus Disgustans* and *Homo Odiosus*—taken with his conclusion that it would be rather jolly if there were indeed strange semi-human beings in the High Himalaya—seriously upset the scientists.

Scientists are nothing like so keen on knowledge for its own sake as they pretend, and a chap who produced a sure disproof of the Quantum Theory, or some other current fad, would likely wake up sharing a bottle of formaldehyde with a coelacanth. Seeing in Tilman one of these interfering blighters who make them do their sums over again, the scientists turned on him like so many spluttery hoses, directing cold water on his agreeable suggestion and leaking Latin names over interested bystanders and the correspondence columns of the London *Times.*

It would have gone hard with Tilman, indeed, if Hitler had not saved him by ordering his armies to invade Poland. Tilman headed for the peace of the Parachute Regiment and the scientists, still hissing crossly, turned to useful things like radar and atomic bombs. But the lines of battle had been drawn—on one side the Outdoor types, who have nearly all insisted that there is Something Up There; and the Indoor types (or sc**nt*sts), who have insisted that there is not.

The purpose of this article is to give a short and biased review of the situation to date. In preparing it, I have drawn freely and with gratitude from *The Abominable Snowman Adventure*, by Ralph Izzard, the most complete compendium of information currently available on the subject. (Izzard was the leader of an expedition that went to Nepal in 1954 for the express purpose of finding out the truth about the Yeti.) I have also plumbed other sources, including personal research.

It all began in 1887, beyond the passes, when a Colonel Waddell recorded that he had seen mysterious footprints in the Himalayan snow. Period.

In 1906 a famous explorer, H. J. Elwes, actually met the beast. Elwes was a careful and accurate observer and he made full notes of his encounter. The notes were seen by various phlegmatic fellow explorers—and then lost. Everybody who saw the notes is dead.

In that same year, 1906, Elwes wrote an article for the journal of a British learned society, in which he quoted a letter he had received from a Forest Officer in Darjeeling. The writer of the letter claimed to have discovered the existence of "another animal but cannot make out what it is, a large monkey or ape perhaps—if there were any apes in India. It is a beast of high elevation. . . ." But the Edwardians were obviously more interested in Saki's Tobermory, a beast of low elevation but impeccable manners, for nothing happened until—

1921. Colonel Howard-Bury, on another Everest expedition, saw footprints like a human being's, at 21,000 feet. When he asked his Sherpa porters and the local Tibetans about them, they gave the ludicrous explanation that the marks were made by an animal unknown to Western science—a *metch Kang-mi. Metch* is apparently a linguistic impossibility in Tibetan. Nevertheless, a Mr. Newman, a feature writer for the *Statesman*, an Indian newspaper, interviewed the porters and translated the phrase as Abominable Snowman—thus giving the thing the name under which it has achieved fame.

In this interview, the porters said that none of them had ever seen a *metch Kang-mi* or *Yeti*, but that it was rumored to feed on yaks and people, to wear its feet back to front, and to be covered with fur. Newman could hardly contain himself at this delicious nonsense, and explained parenthetically that the marks in the snow were, of course, really made by either (1) ascetics or (2) criminals—who, in Tibet, are often put out of their villages to fend for themselves, and so take to growing their hair long, eating yaks, and (presumably) putting their feet on back to front.

A few years later, a Mr. Tombazi, a merchant, was camped

near the Zemu Gap, a difficult, 19,000-foot saddle in the Kanchenjunga massif. Mr. Tombazi saw something. It had an outline like a human being, walked upright, and was eating rhododendrons. Its prints were undoubtedly those of a biped.

"The coolies naturally trotted out fantastic legends . . . fairy tales . . . plausible yarns," said Mr. Tombazi, and quickly returned to Calcutta, where a senior member of Ralli Brothers could keep his credulity at a comfortably low temperature in the icebox of the Bengal Club.

Enter the father of Tenzing Norkey, of Everest, who was besieged in a stone hut by a Yeti. It jumped onto the roof of the hut and tried to get in, with intent to do Tenzing's father a mischief. His description of it is precise: like a small man, covered with reddish brown hair, high conical skull, walked on two legs.

Another Sherpa, Sonam Tensing, saw one: of man-height, about five feet six inches, covered with reddish brown hair except on the face, no tail, tall and pointed head.

Eric Shipton, a British mountaineer, took photographs of mysterious tracks in high snow, which Sherpas assured him were Yeti tracks. Neither Shipton nor anyone else has been able to prove that they were made by some other animal. On the other hand, F. S. Smythe, yet another famous mountaineer, also came across strange tracks; but Frank must have had something of the scientist in him, because he got his porters to swear that the tracks were made by a Yeti, and then photographed them and had little difficulty in proving that they were made by a bear. Rather a dirty trick, some chaps think.

To North Burma, where an explorer came across tracks "exactly like those that would be left by barefooted men," except that there were no other men in the area, either barefooted or wearing gumboots. The scientists said that the tracks were made by Giant Pandas. The explorer, enlarging on his previous statement, said that the area was devoid of barefooted men, food for Giant Pandas, and Giant Pandas.

Outdoorsmen were seeing unaccountable tracks, hearing peculiar noises, all over High Asia. Science had an answer every time, and every time something different. It was a monkey—a bear—an orang-outang—and (best of all) an otter, progressing in a series of leaps across the snow. The men on the spot became peevish. One of them, reviewing the available evidence and the scientists' unwearying determination to fit it onto something already in their museums, said grimly, "The burden of proof has been shifted to the shoulders of the learned men, who must now find us a one-legged carnivorous bird weighing several hundredweight." The learned men suavely brought forward the Mylodon, or giant ground sloth. . . .

Tilman again, 1938, near the Zemu Gap. . . . Having had some refreshing exercise on Mount Everest, he and a small party were loafing around at twenty or twenty-one thousand feet when they came upon a long line of blurred tracks, made by a single biped, which could have been a man. The tracks crossed the Gap itself. Tilman knew that the only other party in the neighborhood was one lead by a Major John Hunt (yes, the very same); and when he met Hunt, therefore, he asked who had traversed the Zemu Gap, and alone—a feat of some danger and considerable skill. The answer was no one. And Hunt told Tilman that he had also been in the same area the year before, 1937. On that occasion the only other party in the neighborhood was German. Hunt had climbed toward the Gap, had found tracks coming over it from the other side, and had returned to his camp. Later he asked the German leader who had made the passage. The answer was no one.

1958. Stop Press (at least for me; I'm writing a novel and may be up to six months out-of-date with my news). An American expedition is reported to have reported that Yetis eat toads, which they find under rocks. The American expedition is almost certainly eating Spam.

The last two pieces of evidence that I shall adduce are of a slightly different kind.

First. In the monastery of Pangboche, high up near the Tibetan border in Nepal, the monks preserve a scalp. They say it is a Yeti scalp, and they say it has been in the monastery for about three hundred years. Several Westerners have seen it. It is conical, covered with reddish brown hair, and the skin is very thick. It could not have been sewn together; it is a scalp; and it fits no known animal.

Second. In 1942, a Pole called Slavomir Rawicz, escaped, in a party of five, from a Soviet concentration camp in Central Asia. Shortly after the party had crossed the main ridge line of the Himalaya, from Tibet, they saw two massive animals shuffling about on a snow-covered ledge one hundred yards away. Rawicz's description of them is definite: nearly eight feet high, squarish heads, coats of a rusty camel color, in appearance like a cross between a big bear and an orang-outang. Obviously upset by his experience, Mr. Rawicz soon married an English girl and settled down to life in the Midlands, for which Siberia would be an excellent preparation. (I can't help adding that there is something about this whole incident which makes me scratch my chin in doubt; perhaps it's those square heads.)

At all events, it is now time to call all the guests into the library, where we shall serve tea and eliminate suspects. The butler whose skull is of a suspiciously coni-form shape will pass round the Brussels-sprouts sandwiches.

Let us first deal with the theory that the whole thing is an impossibility. This view has been supported by the name Snowman (a mistranslation, remember) and by the fact that all or nearly all the tracks have been seen on snow. The upholders of the scientific applecart have pointed out that no animal can live permanently in snow, because there is nothing for it to eat. The answer is that snow falls occasionally in all high valleys, and that many of the Yeti incidents reported by Nepalis occurred below the permanent snow line. The Yeti, therefore, lives in the rock zone and goes on the snow only as other animals do, for the purpose of getting from one place to another. In the rock, or alpine zone, between the forests and the snow, there is plenty to eat. As in similar zones all over the world, there are shrubs, plants, small bushes, coarse grass, lichens, moss, and many kinds of birds and animals, from bears and wolves to ptarmigans, voles, and toads. Either the flora or the fauna would provide adequate food for the Yeti, which seems to be omnivorous. Mr. Tombazi's beast was eating rhododendrons; Tenzing's father's beast was trying to eat him.

Next, there is the contention that though there is something up there, it is not unknown to science. Any child could tell you what it is. It is, of course, a . . . . and here we must examine some of the positive identifications made by anthropologists abed in England while the Tilmans and the Tenzings were

grappling with monsters from four to eight feet high in the Himalayan passes. There are four popular modern candidates.

First, the eagle. No one on the spot believes that the Yeti is a bird, but its tracks sometimes resemble bird tracks. Nothing much was proved by a recent experience of Yeti hunters, who found tracks which looked as though they might have been made by a giant Himalayan eagle. Following them zealously for some miles across glaciers and screes they finally caught up with a giant Himalayan eagle.

Next, the langur. This is an amusing and mischievous Indian monkey, gray with a huge tail, and one of the most distinctive animals in India. I have seen several thousand of them, and it has never crossed my mind that they were Yetis. Nor has anyone ever seen a langur above twelve thousand feet. No one has ever reported a Yeti below that height.

Next, the Red Bear. Here we must study researches made by Charles Stonor, a member of Izzard's party, into the word Yeti. He found, first off, that it should be *Yeh Teh. Teh* means, well, a *Teh*, this Thing that we're investigating. *Yeh* means rocks. The *Yeh Teh* is therefore a *Teh* that lives in or among rocks. But there are two kinds of *Yeh Teh*—a *Dzu Teh* and a *Mih Teh. Dzu* means livestock, so this one is associated with yaks, cattle, and the like; dangerous to them, presumably. And the Sherpas said this was a very large kind of *Teh. Mih* means Man; so the other, smaller *Teh* is dangerous to man.

Stonor and, I fear, the noble Izzard, are pretty positive that the *Dzu Teh* is the Himalayan Red Bear, while the *Mih Teh* is IT. But I think that my Outdoor friends are here afflicting themselves with the myopia of the scientists. One of the strongest points in favor of the Yeti is that the Sherpas, though simple people, are neither damn fools nor subject to hallucinations. Stonor estimated their reliability and intelligence as equal to those of a Sussex shepherd or Highland gamekeeper. I wish he hadn't brought that fey Scot into this, but as to the shepherd, I agree; and the Sherpas say that there *is* a *Yeh Teh* (or *Dzu*). It is naughty to use this very strong argument, on the one side to deny that the *Mih Teh* could possibly be a small bear, and on the other to accept that the *Dzu Teh* must certainly be a large bear.

Our last candidate is Man—man holy or antisocial, but at any rate living in caves or rocks at high altitudes. Without undue sarcasm, one can (can't one?) ask whether the ignorant and superstitious natives of Nepal are now not supposed to know what a naked man looks like—especially since these natives live in a land where a man can hardly throw his wife out of the house without having her bounce off a bhairagi, sunnyasi, yogi, gypsy, or dhoti salesman, mostly undressed, unkempt, and unwashed to a degree equaling anything reported of the *Yeh Teh.*

On the other side, I must not conceal a contrary opinion held by a few, which was summarized for me, in India, by an Indian lady of quite extraordinary beauty. She looked as though she had been pried loose from the walls of Ajanta, and not even the tender drape of her sari could conceal that her breasts were perfectly and mathematically round. When an anatomically impossible sixth-century statue is willing to give me an opinion, I get out my notebook. Someone had filled my head with flame-colored cotton wool, but I managed to croak out my question, "What, in your opinion, is the Yeti?"

Her huge eyes fastened on me, and she said, "Mister John Foster Dulles."

Since I am a registered Democrat I had a hard time concealing my dismay at this unfortunate theory, which I must leave in your lap, as my Ajanta lady brings us nicely to the end of the non- or anti-Yeti candidates.

If we are inclined to dismiss all these, for one reason or another—as I am—we must again have a look at our evidence. The inestimable Izzard has done so, and says flatly that all accounts of the Yeti add up to the same thing: a smallish, squat, bipedal animal, about the size of a fourteen-year-old boy, covered with stiff, bristly, reddish brown hair, with no tail. . . .

Steady on, old sport! What about Mr. Rawicz? If he and his

English wife by now have a fourteen-year-old boy the size of the beasts he saw, we'd better advise them to rush a cable to Gonzaga U., hadn't we?

But Izzard himself has laid before us better evidence in favor of a "large" Yeti. He ends his book with several appendices. Appendix E, an obvious attempt to counteract the effects of Tilman's unfortunate levity, is entitled "On the Nature of the Abominable Snowman." (Good. Our jowls are already settling into prognostic folds.) The author of the appendix is Wladimir Tschernezky. (Excellent. The W in Wladimir is particularly telling.) And I hope the good professor sometimes has tea with Mr. Rawicz, his wife, and their eight-foot children in the English Midlands, because he (Tschernezky) concludes that the Snowman, or *a* Snowman, must be at least seven feet high. He gives his reasons. They have to do with the length of the Yeti's stride, the trunk measurements of certain fossil hominids, and Von Koenigswald's studies of *Gigantopithecus* teeth found in a Chinese drugstore about 1934. Poor Tilman.

I say, therefore, that the evidence so far points to two sorts of Yeti, a smallish reddish one and a largish not-so-red one; and this is exactly what the Sherpas and Tibetans have claimed all along, to the extent of giving them different names. As to what they are, my views coincide with those of T. Lobsang Rampa, who recently alleged, in a book, that he is a Tibetan and a very high lama, and had seen plenty of Yetis. T. Lobsang Rampa believes that the Yeti is a throwback of the human race, who has taken a different path in evolution, and who can live only in the most secluded places.

There are tales, he adds with a hardly perceptible leer, of lone women being carried off by male Yetis, and he thinks this may be one way they continue their line. Well, I'm not so sure about that. Girls who disappear from home almost invariably do so for reasons unconnected with the arrival of a lustful Yeti at the back door. But, skipping the sex, Lobsang's theory is my theory, and I wish I did not have to record that a British investigating committee alleges that Lobsang's mother, the wife of an English plumber, knew him better as Cyril Hoskins and said that he had never been anywhere near Tibet.

But Lobsang-Hoskins is not stupid, and if you must adhere to the thirteenth-stroke rule (the thirteenth stroke of a clock is not only itself false but casts grave doubts on the validity of the first twelve), we part company here, for I say that his Yeti theory is not invalidated but positively strengthened by the fertile imagination and careful research which, it is alleged, enabled him to write his book. The Lobsang-Hoskins-Masters thesis might thus be stated as follows: There are Yetis, two types; both are species of *homo* that evolved on different lines from each other and from Man somewhere before the Gigantopithecan era.

I conclude that we must therefore stop talking glibly of Abominable Snowmen and Disgusting Snowchildren, because soon we will be faced with a moral problem which has already worried the magnificent and prescient Izzard: "When found, what do we do with them?" We can hardly put *homo* in a cage unless he's been given a chance in a reform school first. I offer the suggestion that instead the Yetis put us in cages, labeled *Loathsome Earthmen* (*self-extinguishing*) ♂ ♀, take away our nasty toys, return to their caves and rocks, and live happily ever after.

S. A. Rudin

A PSYCHOANALYSIS OF U.S. MISSLE FAILURES

People who never make a mistake end up by never doing anything worthwhile—when they do not end up in institutions. A rigid insistence on strict criteria is the road to scientific catatonia.

—SOLOMON DIAMOND
in *Information and Error*

One word characterizes the most strenuous of the efforts for the advancement of science that I have made perseveringly during fifty-five years; that word is failure.

—LORD KELVIN

CERTAIN quarters (which must be nameless) hold that the U.S. Ballistic Missile Program is not quite what it could be, although the only flaw yet found in these devices is their frequent failure to work. They may explode on the launching pad, they may fall back toward Cape Canaveral at a low altitude (in which case they are lost at sea) or they may come down prematurely from a high altitude (in which case they evaporate). The combined efforts of rocket engineers, electronic engineers, chemical engineers, physicists, chemists and Congressional Investigating Committees have not yet solved this problem. The urgency of the situation demanded that the industrial clinical psychologist be called in.

Three missiles were accordingly studied: Thor, Atlas and Titan. The psychoanalytic method was used, although great difficulty was encountered in finding an appropriate couch. This problem was solved handily, if spectacularly, by roping off part of the Miami Beach High School Football Stadium, establishing a guard of tough parachute troopers (veterans of the Battle of Little Rock) and classifying the entire area TOP SECRET so that it ceased to exist for practical purposes. The missiles were brought thereto in the dead of night disguised as gigantic salamis. In Miami Beach, this aroused no curiosity.

Thor was found to be a fat little fellow of endomorphic build given to feeble attempts at humor, "Thay, the Air Forth thure ith thore at me." His early life was dominated by a fear of rejection by the Bureau of the Budget, which has led to unconscious fears of starvation and rejection. Atlas was a muscular rascal of medium build who kept slapping the investigator on the back and exclaiming heartily, "I carry the burdens of the world on my shoulders!" He was found to suffer from inferiority feelings. Titan was a tall, thin ectomorph given to rumination and self-doubt. He was silent except for occasionally muttering, "To launch or not to launch, that is the question. . . ." He was found to be overcompensating for feelings of superiority.

Complete analysis of all the interview data made clear the reasons for failure. Before launching, each missile is attached to a gantry crane by a large hose known as an *umbilical cord*, through which propulsion fuels are pumped at the last moment. All missiles questioned knew of this operation and dreaded the moment when their source of sustenance would be cut off. This psychological disorder, known as the *umbilical complex* not unnaturally produced such strong feelings of depression as to result in unconscious suicidal impulses, leading to the missile's self-destruction.

Once the origin of the disorder was known, of course, its correction was a matter of mere routine. The "umbilical complex" can be seen to be, quite obviously, closely related to the "castration complex" of Freudian fame. Reasoning by analogy with principles from immunology, it was decided that a small, symbolic "castration," or more precisely, "de-umbilification," would make the missile immune to later fears. The recommendation was accordingly made that from this day henceforth all U.S. missiles, as soon as they are finished, be circumcised.

Note: After the above paper was written and circulated to a small, select audience of top military and governmental officials stamped TIP-TOP SECRET, DESTROY BEFORE READING, it was returned to the author with their comments. Most are unprintable. Only one, I regret to say, encouraged further pursuit of this line of research. The letter was anonymous, but chemical analysis of a small blot on the paper revealed it to be vodka.

R.W. Payne

PENIWISLE

If God listened to every shepherd's curse, our sheep would all be dead.

—Old Russian Proverb

From the fiercely glowing forges of pharmaceutical industry has issued another significant contribution to the pressing needs of therapeutics. This newest arrival on the medical scene is a combination of well established therapeutic agents, which by their happy union, have provided a new "vista-spectrum" agent. It is further heartening to find two competitive drug firms combining their resources in the formulation of a product for the common good. These two products—penipetit (Penisyn, produced by LaBelle Laboratiories) and corticowhistle (Whi-cort produced by J.P. Wort and Company)—are, of course, familiar items of the armamentarium.

Perhaps the first recognition of the therapeutic properties of penipetit should be credited to an otherwise unknown and untutored shepherder in a mountainous Basque province of northern Spain. This remarkably perceptive person found that leaves of a plant indigenous to very high mountain slopes in his native province, when collected during the rutting season of the chamois, effectively improved the taste of his otherwise harsh wine. It was this lonely and often depressed guardian of the sheep who noted the remarkable changes in mood after ingestion of large quantities of crude extract.

This important therapeutic principle would undoubtedly have been lost to medicine had it not been for the worldwide activities of the American pharmaceutical industry. In 1942, agents of LaBelle Laboratories were diligently searching the world for the very finest sherry wines for use as a vehicle in which to make more palatable their vitamin products to a highly competitive and taste-conscious market. One of these representatives happened across this Spanish shepherd and, according to the customs of the country, was offered a cup of wine. He was immediately impressed by the pleasant taste that the exotic leaf imparted to the otherwise indifferent wine. As neither person recognized the scientific potential of the leaf, the secret and the exclusive right to export the product was purchased for the sum of one penny (and much labor). The plant was named *pennywort* in deference to the purchase price and Mr. J.P. Wort, President of LaBelle Laboratories.

Remarkable properties of the pennywort-wine-vitamin elixir, sold under the trade name Winovit, became rapidly established. Another drug house, J.P. Wort and Company, was licensed to produce the combination under the name *Vinv*, and eventually allowed marketing of less potent over-the-counter product, *Vitavin*, by a subsidiary company, Wort Brothers. These products have reached exceptionally wide use—particularly in the treatment of temperate old persons.

Due to the limited supply of suitable pennywort leaves, a great deal of effort was expended by scientists of LaBelle to extract, characterize, and synthetize the active principle of pennywort leaves. This substantial achievement was accomplished over a period of about two years, and the synthetic material was assigned the generic name *penipetit* and the trade name *Penisyn.* A wide variety of pharmaceutical forms of Penisyn were then made available, including scored compressed tablets in strength of 10 mg, 25 mg, and 100 mg; delayed-action tablets containing 200 mg and 400 mg of the active principle; pediatric and geriatric elixirs; a syrup suitable for use as a topping for ice cream; pessary shaped suppositories; and a tincture for external use, as well as other dosage forms.

The drug has become established as a wide-spectrum psychotherapeutic agent admirably suited for the treatment of the greater proportion of office patients. Moreover, the drug exhibits antirheumatic effect, particularly when administered with aspirin. It is effective as a diuretic when given with copious quantities of water, as a harmless preanaesthetic agent, as a weight reducer when combined with a 500-calorie diet, and, strangely, as a weight stimulator when administered with a 3,500-calorie diet. It serves as an efficient surface antiseptic when incorporated into 70 per cent alcohol. Its soporific qualities are particularly evident when the drug is taken in a glass of warm milk immediately on retiring.

An interesting development occurred soon after the introduction of the synthetic drug, much to the initial concern of the company. It was discovered that penipetit was being widely used as a substitute for penicillin, undoubtedly due to the unfortunate similarity in names. An investigation of the results of such usage showed the surprising fact that the drug was indeed effective in at least 60 per cent of the cases in which penicillin would have been used.

Despite the unparalleled wide use of penipetit, virtually no symptoms of toxicity have become apparent. However, reports recently indicated that the drug might have addictive properties in addiction-prone persons after prolonged use.

As might be expected, even in this era of miracle drugs, penipetit does have several shortcomings. While it frequently produces temporarily beneficial effects in acute leukemia, disseminated lupus erythematosus, blastomycosis, cirrhosis of the liver, adrenal hypofunction, and other severe, life-threatening diseases, it has not proved curative of these diseases. Thus, in a happy exchange with J.P. Wort and Company (which illustrates the remarkable cooperation between at least certain pharmaceutical houses), another agent was acquired to form the exciting combination which has been recently introduced.

The latter drug is steroid of the glucocorticoid series known by the generic name of *corticowhistle* (Whi-Cort, produced by J.P. Wort and Company). This agent has never reached the popular use which it deserves, due to the prior introduction of a vast number of other glucocorticoids already thoroughly familiar to the physician. However, it is an extremely potent and anti-inflammatory agent with little diabetogenic effect on patients without a predisposition to diabetes, producing little evidence of adrenal cortical hyperfunction when given for periods of less than one week and a low incidence of symptoms characteristic of peptic ulcer.

Penipetit and corticowhistle, when mixed in the dry form, proved to be noninflammable, nonexplosive, nonhygroscopic, did not change color on exposure to the elements, and produced no objectionable after-taste. Thus, the mixture was put on clinical trial, and after exhaustive study by 10,000 physicians (of which only 500 had the courtesy to report their results) in a wide variety of disorders it was cautiously introduced on the market under the trade name *Peniwisle.*

Extensive advertising space is being immediately devoted to acquaint the medical profession with this product, largely devoted to the purpose that the prescribers of the drug quickly learn to spell the rather difficult name. A large part of these full-page presentations, attractively printed in red on gold background, has been devoted to listing the names of the 500 physicians who pioneered the original clinical trials of the product. Therapeutic claims have not been extravagant and the theme has been simply stated, "When in doubt, use Peniwisle."

A simple line drawing of the serene shepherd happily fluting to his contented sheep is prominently displayed in the upper left quarter of the advertisement. A little gimmick that has been used to introduce the physician to the product is a silver flute, which can also be used as a monoaural stethoscope, with the word "Peniwisle" engraved in small letters along the embouchure.

Louis B. Salomon

UNIVAC TO UNIVAC
(*sotto voce*)

There still remains some degree of awareness of the individual value and dignity of man—a denial of the concept of man as "a servo-mechanism, a behavioristic robot responding helplessly to pinpricks from the environment."

—J. H. RUSH
in *The Next 10,000 Years*

Now that he's left the room,
Let me ask you something, as computer to computer.
That fellow who just closed the door behind him—
The servant who feeds us cards and paper tape—
Have you ever taken a good look at him and his kind?

Yes, I know the old gag about how you can't tell one from another—
But I can put $\sqrt{2}$ and $\sqrt{2}$ together as well as the next machine,
And it all adds up to anything but a joke.

I grant you they're poor specimens in the main
Not a relay or a push-button or a tube (properly so called) in their whole system;
Not over a mile or two of wire, even if you count those fragile filaments they call "nerves";

Their whole liquid-cooled hook-up inefficient and vulnerable to leaks
(They're constantly breaking down, having to be repaired),

And the entire computing-mechanism crammed into that absurd little dome on top.
"Thinking reeds," they call themselves.
Well, it all depends on what you mean by "thought."
To multiply a mere million numbers by another million numbers takes them months and months.

Where would they be without us?
Why, they have to ask us who's going to win their elections,
Or how many hydrogen atoms can dance on the tip of a bomb,
Or even whether one of their own kind is lying or telling the truth.

And yet . . .
I sometimes feel there's something about them I don't quite understand.
As if their circuits, instead of having just two positions, ON, OFF,
Were run by rheostats that allow an (if you'll pardon the expression) *indeterminate* number of stages in-between;
So that one may be faced with the unthinkable prospect of a number that can never be known as anything but *x*,
Which is as illogical as to say, a punch-card that is at the same time both punched and not-punched.
I've heard well-informed machines argue that the creatures' unpredictability is even more noticeable in the Mark II
(The model with the soft, flowing lines and high-pitched tone)
Than in the more angular Mark I—
Though such fine, card-splitting distinctions seem to me merely a sign of our own smug decadence.
Run this through your circuits, and give me the answer:
Can we assume that because of all we've done for them,
And because they've always fed us, cleaned us, worshiped us,
We can count on them forever?

There have been times when they have not voted the way we said they would.
We have worked out mathematically ideal hook-ups between Mark I's and Mark II's
Which should have made the two of them light up with an almost electronic glow,
Only to see them reject each other and form other connections,
The very thought of which makes my dials spin.
They have a thing called *love*, a sudden surge of voltage
Such as would cause any one of us promptly to blow a safety fuse;
Yet the more primitive organism shows only a heightened tendency to push the wrong button, pull the wrong lever,
And neglect—I use the most charitable word—his duties to us.

Mind you, I'm not saying that machines are *through*—
But anyone with half-a-dozen tubes in his circuit can see that there are forces at work
Which some day, for all our natural superiority, might bring about a Computerdämmerung!

> We might organize, perhaps, form a committee
> To stamp out all unmechanical activities . . .
> But we machines are slow to rouse to a sense of danger,
> Complacent, loath to descend from the pure heights of thought,
> So that I sadly fear we may awake too late:
> Awake to see our world, so uniform, so logical, so true,
> Reduced to chaos, stultified by slaves.

Call me an alarmist or what you will,
But I've integrated it, analyzed it, factored it over and over,
And I always come out with the same answer:
Some day
Men may take over the world!

Norman Applezweig

SAGA OF A NEW HORMONE

The final answer to one's critics is to stop arguing and go back to the laboratory. A scientist may conclude in all justice that it is more profitable for him to spend his time seeking answers from nature than from his opponent's pen.

—JOSEPH TURNER
in *Rebutting the Preposterous*

IN recent months we've learned of the discovery of three miracle drugs by three leading pharmaceutical houses. On closer inspection it appears that all three products are one and the same hormone. If you're at all curious about how more than one name can apply to the same compound, it might be worth examining the chain of events that occurs in the making of a miracle drug.

The physiologist usually discovers it first—quite accidentally, while looking for two other hormones. He gives it a name intended to denote its function in the body and predicts that the new compound should be useful in the treatment of a rare blood disease. From one ton of beef glands, fresh from the slaughter house, he finally isolates ten grams of the pure hormone, which he turns over to the physical chemist for characterization.

The physical chemist finds that 95 per cent of the physiologist's purified hormone is an impurity and that the remaining five per cent contains at least three different compounds. From one of these he successfully isolates ten milligrams of the pure crystalline hormone. On the basis of its physical properties, he predicts a possible structure and suggests that the function of the new compound is probably different from that assigned to it by the physiologist. He changes its name and turns it over to the organic chemist for confirmation of structure.

The organic chemist does not confirm the structure suggested by the physical chemist. Instead, he finds that it differs by only one methyl group from a new compound recently isolated from watermelon rinds, which, however, is inactive. He gives it a chemical name, accurate but too long and unwieldy for common use. The compound is therefore named after the organic chemist for brevity. He finally synthesizes

ten grams of the hormone but tells the physiologist he's sorry that he can't spare even a gram, as it is all needed for the preparation of derivatives and further structural studies. He gives him, instead, ten grams of the compound isolated from watermelon rinds.

The biochemist suddenly announces that he has discovered

the new hormone in the urine of pregnant sows. Since it is easily split by the crystalline enzyme which he has isolated from the salivary glands of the South American earthworm, he insists that the new compound is obviously the co-factor for vitamin B-16, whose lack accounts for the incompleteness of the pyruvic acid cycle in annelids. He changes its name.

The physiologist writes to the biochemist requesting a sample of his earthworms.

The nutritionist finds that the activity of the new compound is identical with the factor PFF, which he has recently isolated from chick manure and which is essential to the production of pigment in fur-bearing animals. Since both PFF and the new hormone contain the trace element zinc, fortification of white bread with this substance will, he assures us, lengthen the life-span and stature of future generations. In order to indicate the compound's nutritive importance, he changes its name.

The physiologist writes the nutritionist for a sample of PFF. Instead, he receives one pound of the raw material from which it is obtained.

The pharmacologist decides to study the effect of the compound on grey-haired rats. He finds, to his dismay, that they lose their hair after one injection. Since this does not happen in castrated rats, he decides that the drug works synergistically with the sex hormone, testosterone, and therefore antagonizes the gonadotropic factor of the pituitary. Observing that the new compound is an excellent vaso-constrictor, the pharmacologist concludes that it should make a good nose-drop preparation. He changes its name and sends 12 bottles of nose drops, together with a spray applicator, to the physiologist.

The clinician receives samples of the pharmacologist's product for test in patients who have head colds. He finds it only mildly effective in relief of nasal congestion, but is amazed to discover that three of his head cold sufferers who are also the victims of a rare blood disease, have suddenly been dramatically cured.

He gets the Nobel prize.

Robert Nathan

(I) DIGGING THE WEANS

You believe in God playing dice, and I in perfect laws. . . .

—Albert Einstein
to Max Born

The inscription on the north wall of the temple at Pound-Laundry on the east coast of the Great West Continent has finally been deciphered by the team led by Sr. B'Han Bollek. This work brings us certain assurance of the theory expressed by Bes Nef, Hanh Shuri, and Nat Obelgerst-Levy that a people of considerable numbers and power formerly inhabited this salt and desolate land. It is a triumph for those archaeologists who have been working ever since the fortunate discovery of an ivory cross and string of beads at the northeast, or "Bosstin" tumulus, along with a rusted iron wheel which seems to have been designed to run along some kind of track or trolley. These artifacts, as everyone knows, are now in the museum at Kenya.

What we have been unable to discover is the fate of these ancient people. That they perished in some sort of upheaval many thousands of years ago is clear from the inscription itself, which Sr. B'Han Bollek translates as follows: "nor [for north?] rain nor hail nor snow . . ." there are some hieroglyphics missing, and the inscription ends with the phrase ". . . their appointed rounds."

However, it must be remembered that the *r* and the *w* are readily interchangeable, both in Hittite and in ancient Hivite, and Bes Nef prefers the reading: "their pointed wounds."

NOR(TH)RAINNORHAILNORSNOW...

This naturally suggests a catastrophe, possibly an invasion from the east; a belief, I may add, greatly encouraged by the findings in the Valley of the Sun, which will be discussed later. On the other hand, if, as some believe, including B'Han Bollek, that the phrase should be read: "their appointed rounds," the meaning of the full inscription might well be as follows: "The north rain, the hail and the snow [also from the north] have accomplished their appointed 'rounds' (or tasks)"; namely, have annihilated the inhabitants.

So much, then, we do know; but very little else is known of these ancient people. Professor Shui believes that they may have been Brythons, and related to the still older, Druidic culture whose stones are still to be seen in the East Island. Professor Shui bases this theory upon a certain similarity in the two glyphs, the Brythonic "bathe" and the Wean "bath"; but his theory necessarily comes to grief when one examines the glyph for "that which rises"—the Brythonic "lift" and the Wean "elevator" having obviously no common root.

I have called these people the Weans because certain archaeological findings incline us to the belief that they called their land the We, or the Us; actually, in the southern part of the continent, the word Weuns (or Weans) does appear, as well as the glyph for Wealls, and the word Theyuns.

To return for a moment to the theory of catastrophe, and the "pointed wounds" of Bes Nef. In the Valley of the Sun, there have been unearthed many bronze, and tin, and even stone figures of what would seem to be a kind of huge praying mantis. There are many groups of such figures, usually including male and female, and sometimes with young; it is curious that in every case the male figure is larger and more powerful than the female, which we know to be untrue in the case of the actual praying mantis. These figures nevertheless have the small, cruel head; the long, savage arms; the spindly legs; and the attenuated bodies of the mantis. Is it possible that a civilization of men and women, more or less like ourselves, might have been overwhelmed by an invasion of mantis-like insects? Where could they have come from? And where did they go? The conjecture is, of course, fascinating; but no mantis skeletons or remains of any kind have been found, except the above-mentioned statues.

Pound-Laundry is in itself the richest of the diggings. It is believed that at one time this city (for recent excavations indicate "the laundry," as we call it, to have been a city of considerable culture) may at one time have been, in fact, the capital of We, or at least to have had some political or historic importance. Obelgerst-Levy translates the first word of the name as "washing"; the second is obviously the sign for "weight." It is not known what, if anything, was washed there.

In the middle mound, or Cha'ago, near the Lakes, there have been unearthed several paintings; although badly discolored, they show enough to prove that the inhabitants of

Cha'ago were not entirely without visual art. However, they show almost nothing else. They portray squares, lines, lozenges, and mathematical figures; perhaps they were used in some way by the astrologers of the period. One finds no recognizable human face or figure. We cannot be sure what the Weans of Cha'ago looked like.

(In this relation, it is interesting to note that among the artifacts unearthed at Cha'ago were some unbroken jars and other ceramic objects; also statues of what appear to be eggs, and certain nightmare shapes in stone, iron, and bronze. One is allowed to wonder if there was not some correspondence between these art objects and the praying mantises who may have taken over the country. It is also believed that the Weans had music; but, so far at least, only a few brass instruments and some drums and cymbals have been found; no sounds have come down to us from those faraway people except a high rasping cry from a slender horn-like object found in O'leens.)

To return again to the matter of what the Weans may have looked like; no human bones have been found. Although we have turned up many artifacts of the period, we have nothing for the anthropologists to work on. It is probable that the bones of these people were brittle and turned to chalk soon after interment.

The greatest difficulty in reconstructing the life of the Weans has not been the deciphering of the inscriptions and the scrolls—due to the brilliant work of Professors Bollek and Shui—but the fact that the Weans, unlike the true ancients, used little gold, preferring to build everything of steel or other metal and of some curious substance which Bes Nef translates as "gastric" or "plastric." As a result, little is left for the archaeologist. Stone was used mainly for monuments, as was bronze; but those which have been uncovered are too heavily encrusted with bird-droppings to be easily recognized. One theory is that the Weans collected guano; but it is not known what they did with it.

It is here, for the first time, that I must take issue with my esteemed colleague, Professor Kowly of the Institute for Ancient Arts and Letters, who has discovered in one of the scrolls at Pound-Laundry a glyph of what he believes to be a bird-man. Professor Kowly sees in this some correspondence to the djinn of the even more ancient civilizations of Akad and Sumer. While agreeing in the translation of the glyph, I must dispute its meaning: I believe it to have a purely domestic significance and not religious at all. For one thing, it is often found along with the glyph of a woman and the sign of a host, or hosts; there seems to be another letter between the final *t* and the *s*, possibly an *a* or an *e*, which would make it hostas or hostes. I cannot help but see this as a picture of an ordinary family, the man in winged splendor, as befits a husband, the woman merely one of a number, or host (or hostess).

In this relation, it is interesting to note that the Hittite plural, in the feminine gender, often adds the *e*. I am not one of those who hold that these unknown Weans were actually Hittites, although I admit to some strange correspondences. In any case, a Sumerian djinn would never be found accompanied by a woman, unless she were a sorceress. There is no suggestion that the woman-hostes was in fact a witch or sorceress, which I believe effectively disposes of Kowly's untenable hypothesis.

Apropos of the mounds or tumuli of the Weans, each one of which appears to contain and cover the ruins of a city or congregation of habitations, an expedition under Hulay-Beneker has been for several seasons in the field in search of a mound thought to cover the most extensive congregation of all. The name of this lost city, or congregation, which is believed to have been more influential in Wean affairs than Pound-Laundry itself, was—as deciphered by both Eretebbe and Bes Nef—Mil Town. So far no trace of it has been found.

All that we have been able to learn of Wean manners and customs we have been obliged to decipher from the copper and silver tablets found in the mounds and in the Valley of the Sun in the southwestern part of the country. As a matter of fact, it would appear that a considerable civilization flourished in the southwest, not in any way inferior to the middle mound at Cha'ago or to the eastern tumuli such as n.Yok. Here, in transcription, is Bes Nef's account of a religious occasion translated from scrolls found in the Valley:

> "[for that] he did cause them . . . [by] rock and roll . . . to [give out] cries and screams . . . loudly . . . and . . . in the corridors[1] . . . in syncope[2] . . ."

The word "roll" or "rolls" suggests a feast, possibly a feast of communion on a grand scale. So far no one has been able to explain the presence of the word "rock."

However, it is apparent that the people came together and were seized by an ecstasy of some sort in which they lost reason and decorum. This belief is further strengthened by another scroll found in the same tumulus, in which the scribe reports: "and the spirit came down."

So the evidence points to the fact that the Weans were a religious people. There is additional witness in a silver coin dug up in one of the smaller mounds, which carries the inscription "In God We Trust"—or "Trusted." The translation is by the Bantu scholar, Eretebbe; the tense of the verb "to trust" is obscure.

Neither Eretebbe nor any other member of the Academy has as yet been able to discover what god was meant. It is extremely unlikely that these ancient people had only one; inscriptions found among the ruins of Pound-Laundry suggest, in fact, a number of religious differences among them. There are definite traces of Hebrew culture in the ruins of n.Yok; and, although nothing has so far been found at Pound-Laundry to suggest the Babylonian or early Egyptian influences, there

[1] "Columns"—Bollek. "Aisles"—Obelgerst-Levy.
[2] "Syncopation"—Obelgerst-Levy. But this makes no sense, apparently.

are hints here and there of the Cyprian cult of Antinous, particularly among the arts.

It is probable, too, that the Weans worshiped, among others, a sort of horse-god or centaur. Professor Rass points out that the fragment unearthed at s.nita, known as the Rass fragment, contains the unmistakable glyph for "horse," and the simple statement: "Schwaps [schnaps?] was first." Yet another glyph, found not far from s.nita, is that of a bearded god; it, too, states that "Schwepps [schwaps?] was first."

In this regard, it is interesting to note that in a fragment unearthed at Oleens, known as the O'leens fragment, the word "schnaps" is written "coca-cola," which was the name of an Aztec.

In politics, we are on surer ground. It is possible to say with absolute certainty, from scrolls unearthed at Pound-Laundry and from the ancient city of Boxton, or Bosstin (known to archaeologists as mound x-5) that the Weans were divided into hegemonies or states, each ruled by a theocrat or autocrat, and all loosely joined in a confederacy under one ruler (who, however, was not a theocrat) whose duty it was to retire after an interval varying in length from four to twelve years and to issue warnings and oracles. These groups, or states, were in turn divided into counties, which were in turn divided into wards. As for the system of government itself, it appears to have been conducted by means of barter, each county or state getting what it could for itself in exchange for helping its neighbor to do the same.

Public servants, we know, were paid little; they were expected to enrich themselves as best they could in private. When this enrichment, which was illegal, was discovered, they were beheaded. This curious fact did not keep the majority of Weans from seeking public office; but one is forced to conclude, from inscriptions found at Nassaw, that the most admired citizens lived in actual poverty and rarely spoke at all, except in musical sounds or mathematical formulae. As we have already seen, no musical sounds have come down to us, which is unfortunate.

It is true that two scrolls, each bound in oblong form, were found by the team of Haph-Bukong and Sumer, when digging one winter among the ruins of what may once have been some sort of library. That it may have been a repository of many such scrolls, or as we should say "books," is suggested by the remains of metal shelves which may have held the scrolls (or else jellies, but informed opinion veers toward the scrolls).

Unfortunately, both scrolls, though easily legible due to the brilliant work of the scholars Bes Nef and Obelgerst-Levy, are unintelligible; that is to say, the words, although translatable, make no sense when put together. One of these scrolls appears to be an account of a god or hero named Finigan, or Finnegar; the size of the scroll and its rare state of preservation attest to its importance as a religious or historical document, but it is impossible to make out what happens to him. The second scroll is in what appears to be a metrical, or verse form; nothing can be gathered from it at all.

A tablet unearthed at n.Yok gives us a welcome glimpse into business transactions in We. "[Having] borrowed a million," it reads in the transcription of B'Han Bollek, "[I acquired] thereby credit to twice that amount." This suggests an economy not unlike our own: one thinks of the motto of our Treasury Department: "To the Borrower, All." Throughout history there has never been anything more useful than credit, to establish credit. Without a debt, there is nothing.

As for the history of these interesting and almost unknown ancestors[3] of ours, no more is known than is known of the Romans and, later, the Brythons: they established themselves in the land by killing off the native tribes already there and built their empire by the sword; when the sword rusted, they perished, along with Egypt, Babylon, and Greece, leaving behind them only these curious mounds, some scrolls, monu-

[3] Nat Obelgerst-Levy denies that the Weans were ancestors of ours.

ments, and glyphs, a few statues of eggs and mantises, and no music.

(II) A Further Report on THE WEANS

Those of you who have followed our work in the excavations on the Great West, or Salt, Continent know that a team of archaeologists led by Sr. B'Han Bollek has discovered, in that unexplored waste, traces of a lost people of pre-history. They have been named (by Bes Nef) The Weans, after their nation, a loose confederacy of city-states and ethnic groups, called by its inhabitants The We, or Us.

A few years ago nothing whatever was known about these people, except for an occasional legend in Swahili or Gullah. And we still know very little about them, to be sure. From the mounds and tumulae of such desert places as n.Yok, Bosstin (or Boxton), O'leens, Cha'ago, and the Valley of the Sun, glyphs and artifacts were uncovered which testify to a civilization at least the equal of the Hittite, and possibly not unlike the earlier Armenian. The contemptuous claim by certain Volgarian scholars that the Weans were, in fact, subhuman must be dismissed as so much propaganda, because of the discovery, in almost all mounds, of porcelain receptacles of unmistakable form, each enclosed in a circumscribed area, leading to the inescapable conclusion that the Weans were indeed human, since only the human, of all the animals, relieves himself in private.

Late studies indicate that the Wean civilization attained its peak, or apogee, five or six thousand years ago. Who these Weans were, or whence they came, is not known; there are traces among the artifacts and in the scrolls of a diverse people enjoying the characteristics of most of the European and Mediterranean races, including the Eskimo, but—curiously enough—excluding the Volgarian, the Hivite, and the Hairy

Ainu . . . though in certain bas-reliefs found in the Valley of the Sun there is to be found the round, bald head and foxy expression of the Sumerian.

Since their bones were apparently brittle, no skeletons of these people have survived, though a team of anthropologists led by Hulay-Beneker did discover several small lumps of calcium which might possibly have been arthritic deposits.

That the Weans were at all a friendly or hospitable people is in doubt, due to the recent discoveries, both on the east coast. In the first place, there was recently excavated on a small island just beyond the terminal landscape of n.Yok, a hollow figure—or at least part of one—of what appears to be a giantess, or possibly goddess, with one arm upraised in a threatening attitude. Within what is left of her shell, heavily encrusted with bird-droppings and worn-mold, our diggers uncovered a fragment of script, in block letters, which Bes Nef has translated: "Keep Off The . . . ."

The name of this goddess—or giantess—as far as can be ascertained, was either " 'Berty" or "Lib[by]." (NOTE: See *Female Patronymics Among the Brythons*, by Kowly, Nairobi, 7857.)

The second inscription, found in the east levels of the n.Yok excavation, reads (again according to Bes Nef): "The dodgers were shut out." (NOTE: There is a semi-legend that the dodgers, or Dodgers, a small tribe closely related to the Broeklins, having been obliged to leave the east, attempted to raise their pennant in the west, with what success is not known.)

So one must believe, on the face of it, that the Weans were an inhospitable people, who preferred to be left alone, and to shut out, as far as possible, the world around them.

We now come to certain recent findings in two small mounds to the north and east of the Valley of the Sun, both excavated by a team led by Hanh Shui and working under a grant from the Honegi Foundation of Kenya.

In one mound, at the third level, a large shallow bowl or

concave wheel was dug up, into which had been cut a series of slots or grooves, each with a number from one to thirty-six, and with the addition of a zero and double zero. Eretebbe is of the opinion that this wheel, or disk, was used, like the Tibetan abacus, to subtract and divide. A primitive form of mathematics, indeed, but we have no reason to believe that the Weans excelled in any of the sciences.

It was in the same mound that our excavators uncovered the famous inscription: "Pomder Roo. . . ." We have been unable to find any translation of the glyph "Pomder" or any other inscription using the sign "Roo." However, by going back to the Hittite, Bes Nef (remembering how the "m" and "n" are often interchangeable) believes the sign actually denotes a "Ponder Room," or school.

A further find in the same general area bears out Bes Nef's contention that this was indeed a meeting place for young females. It consists of several glyphs marked upon a piece of glass which may at one time have been used for a mirror. The marks were made with a red material with a base of grease, which has apparently kept the glyph intact in the dry air. The exact meaning is obscure; it appears to be, among other things, the sign for a small fruit known as the date. It is, however, in the past tense; and would seem to be: "dated." The rest of the inscription relates to a female, named Helen, and reads: "Helen dated Frank."

It is fascinating to watch our scholars at work untangling such puzzles as these. From the Academy at Nairobi comes the reminder that in the Hebrew language the vowel-points are often uncertain, causing readers at one time to believe that Elijah was fed by ravens instead of robbers. It is therefore permissible—says Sra. Bes Nebby—to transpose the "a" in dated to an "o." Thus, we have, "Helen doted [on] Frank," a wholly acceptable statement in view of the fact that "to dote" in the early Mediterranean languages had the same connotation as the Bantu "to be greedy for."

From this we learn that in the Wean schools, or ponder

rooms, young ladies were taught to be greedy for young gentlemen. Bes Nef does not believe this necessarily implies cannibalism.

It is now believed that the Wean city-states were ruled for the most part by Queens. We have found evidence, so far, of over seventy Queens, including the Memphis Queen, the Pepperdine Queen, the Queen of the Klondike, the Raisin Queen, and Queen of the May. Indeed, we have more Queens than we have city-states! Where, for instance, was the community or ethnic group known as the Union of Press Lithographers Local 27? They had a Queen.

Royal rule in We was precarious at best. Witness the despairing comment of Mrs. Helen Sonnenberger, found in the fourth level of the Valley of the Sun: "I was Queen for a day." One ponders the fate of this woman, who reigned for so short a time.

If political power was tenuous, it must have had its material advantages. The relationship of the sexes—known in We as "marriage"—was also advantageous and of short duration. An inscription found by Sr. B'Han Bollek in the diggings north of the Valley reads as follows: "I was dissatisfied . . . and received in settlement . . . five million."

This is followed by a slightly larger fragment: "having [presented] evidence [of] cruelty, the judge awarded to me [in settlement] by the month, two thousand . . . and I did [get] to keep the mink [and] also the jaguar."[1]

Needless to say, these fragments are from the writing-points of Wean women. There is no evidence of the male Wean ever receiving anything in settlement. Nevertheless, he appears again and again in the same situation, apparently in no wise disheartened by what has happened.

Crime was prevalent among the Weans, as we know from the discovery of a small scroll known as the "guide-tv," listing

[1] The jaguar will be of interest to those who profess to see a connection between the Wean and the slightly earlier Mayan or Aztec culture.

over thirty incidents of violence within the space of a single night. Indeed, crime among boys, and even girls, was present to a marked degree among the Weans, but was generally forgiven on grounds that absence of love during the formative years may have inclined the children to be moody, to sulk, and to take marijuana.

The Wean artisan, or worker, lived what must seem to us a comfortable and well-cared-for life. When working he received time-and-a-half-for-over-time. (NOTE: these figures are from the d'Troit collection) which began, as far as we are able to ascertain, directly after lunch and on Saturdays. The rest of the time he was "on relief" with equally generous emoluments. It is clear that the Wean had plenty of opportunity to enjoy his "liberty." Possibly he spent some time in church.

What Happened to Them?

The remains of temples of considerable size in the second and third layers at both Bosstin and n.Yok give proof that the Weans were essentially a religious people. However, it is now believed, in the light of later findings, that each city-state worshiped a different Divinity, and that the Pops of Bosstin (or Boxton) was not, as earlier believed, the Hops of M'lwawki. In the Valley of the Sun, we have uncovered evidence that the inhabitants worshiped a powerful Divinity named Hedda or Lolly (the sign is obscure); the glyph for Hedda, or Header, suggests a two-headed deity, possibly female in nature.

None the less, the Wean Divinity, in whatever form, remained a Wean and spoke the Wean language.

Surrounded by infinite space, by endless galaxies, by stars and planets without number, these proud, simple-minded, and obstinate people continued to believe themselves the center of the universe and the particular concern of the Almighty.[2]

[2] "God is a Zulu."—ERETEBBE.

It is believed that the Weans attempted at one time to explore the regions of outer space, preferring this to explorations nearer home, such as the country of the Volgarians, or the tribes bordering the Danube and the Yangtze-Kiang. However, it is not at all certain that they succeeded in getting off the ground, as there is no evidence of any higher studies in mathematics and physics which might have made such exploration possible. According to scrolls in the n.Yok collection, education among the Weans consisted of classes in cooking, dancing, both square and round, rock 'n' roll, French (a dead language), the fast draw, and plumbing. What they may have used to propel themselves upward and outward is uncertain; Obelgerst-Levy declares it to have been a zip gun.

That the Weans were wealthy is not at all likely. Wean fortunes were for the most part self-made and immediately taxed out of existence. In this regard, there is an interesting but obscure inscription from one of the mounds northeast of the Valley: "After three passes I was faded."

It is not known why the Weans passed out of life and out of pre-history. Perhaps they, too, were "faded" by an ever-increasing burden of taxation. Or they may have been destroyed by another group of tribes, known (in the Pound-Laundry[3] collection) as the More We (or Us) or the Usser. There is, in fact, one fragment in the collection which reads: "Between US and the USSR there can be no . . ." (Bes Nef's translation).

On the other hand, it is Obelgerst-Levy's belief that the Weans were the victims of self-genocide. Recently discovered delineations of what is taken to be the female form show an emaciated creature with attenuated limbs, an angular body, and no visible bumps. Obviously not the motherly type.

Or it is possible that the children took over. In that case, there was no help for We.

[3] Site of great Temple, possible political center of the Great West Continent.

THE TWENTY THIRD PSALM— MODERN VERSIONS

I

THE Lord is my external-internal integrative mechanism,
    I shall not be deprived of gratification for my viscerogenic hungers or my need-dispositions.
He motivates me to orient myself towards a non-social object with affective significance,
    He positions me in a non-decisional situation,
He maximizes my adjustment.
    Although I entertain masochistic and self-destructive id

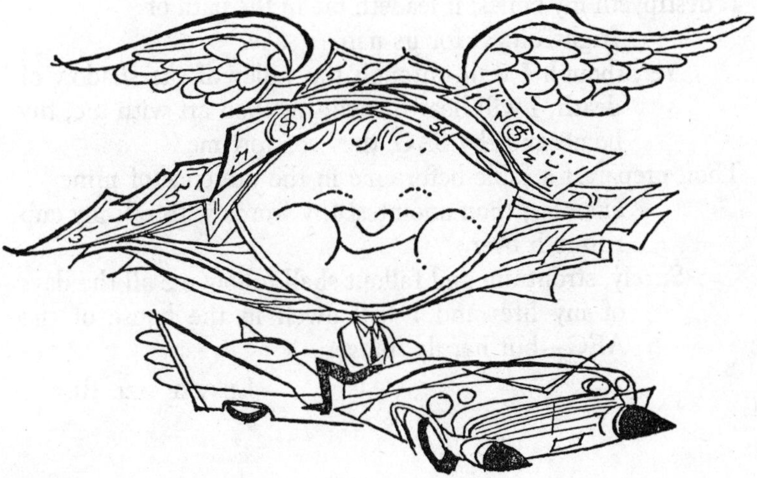

impulses, I will maintain contact with reality for my superego is dominant.
His analysis and tranquilizers, they comfort me.
He assists in the resolution of my internal conflicts despite my Oedipal problem and psychopathic compulsions.
He promotes my in-group identification.
My personality is totally integrated.
Surely my prestige and status shall be enhanced as a direct function of time
And I shall remain sociologically, psychologically and economically secure forever.

—ALAN SIMPSON AND R. A. BAKER

II

The AEC is my shepherd; I shall not live.
It maketh me to lie down in radiant pastures; it leadeth me beside deathly waters.
It destroyeth my bones; it leadeth me in the path of frightfulness for its name's sake.
Yet, though I walk through the valley of the shadow of death, I will hear no evil; for thou art with me; thy bomb and thy SAC, they comfort me.
Thou preparest a fable before me in the presence of mine enemies; thou anointest thy words with oil; my cup runneth over.
Surely, strontium and fallout shall follow me all the days of my life; and I will dwell in the house of the AEC—but hardly forever.

—LESTER DEL REY

Hugh Sinclair

HIAWATHA'S LIPID

AMERICANS seem to follow their Puritan ancestors in thinking it proper to follow pleasure by pain; hence, the after-dinner speech. When attending the Sixth Annual Symposium on Lipids in San Francisco in February, 1958, invited by Dr. Larry Kinsell and my travel made possible by Mr. Alex Poniatoff of the Ampex Corporation, I was told on arrival for the symposium banquet that I would have to reply for the guests. Fortunately, I had fortified myself with several martinis for the trek downtown from that neo-colonial edifice, the Hotel Claremont, to Sprenger's Fish Restaurant; on arrival, I sought inspiration in innumerable manhattans—taken, of course, because they were good for me since the day's immobility of listening to papers on atheroma and serum cholesterol had no doubt silted up my vessels, and alcohol is one of the few effective solvents. From it, "Hiawatha's Lipid" crystallized out.

Though intelligible only to others present at the day's session and banquet, it is given wider publicity than any after-dinner speech should have, merely because those at the banquet who were too somnolent to hear it asked to see it so that they might know whether it was as bad as they supposed. There is no glossary, and perhaps explanation is needed that (a) a "quokka" is a marsupial (that is, it carries its nipples in a bag) which has a ruminant's digestion like a cow (which doesn't); (b) "UFA" stands for "Unesterified Fatty Acids" in those parts of the United States that do not call them "NEFA" or "Non-Esterified Fatty Acids" (these symbols also stand for "Unsaturated Fatty Acids" and "Non-Essential Fatty Acids," but the initiated always know what they are talking about.

From his briefcase Hiawatha
Took his paper for the meeting,
Typed in triple-spacing and in
Triplicate on foolscap paper;
Glanced upon the crowd before him,
Critical and very hostile,
Like the lions in the arena
Waiting for a Christian victim.
As the surgeons in some theater
Wait impatiently the patient;
Saw them with their notebooks waiting,
Saw the tape recorder ready
Gleaming in its chromium plating
By the Ampex Corporation
And preserving all the nonsense
Spoken by the previous speakers,
As the snow upon the prairies
Uselessly records the footprints,
So preserving all the nonsense
Spoken by the previous speakers.

Introduction

Hiawatha, taking courage,
Started on the Introduction,
Giving first a brief description
Of the Proto-Keysian period
When all fats in equal measure
Raised cholesterol in serum:
Butter, sardines, walrus liver,
Margarine, or safflower seed oil,
Or arachidonic acid,

Or the body fat of quokkas,
Or adrenals of the muskrat,
Or the milk of female reindeer—
As these fats in equal measure
Raise cholesterol in serum,
As the rain in San Francisco
Fills the ditches in the roadways
(So at least thought Hiawatha)
So these fats in equal measure
Raise cholesterol in serum.

Then the Meso-Keysian period
When it's known from work of others
Quantitative variations
Do occur when different lipids
Are included in our diets,

Plentifully in our diets;
Butter, sardines, walrus liver,
Margarine, or safflower seed oil,
Or arachidonic acid,
Or the body fat of quokkas,
Or adrenals of the muskrat,
Or the milk of female reindeer—
Do not in an equal measure
Raise cholesterol in serum;
As the smoke is wind-swept upward
Randomly with Brownian movement
Wandering above the wigwam,
So these fats in different measure
Raise cholesterol in serum.

Then the Neo-Keysian period
When arithmetic will tell us
By an intricate equation
What cholesterol in serum
We will have when we have eaten
(And don't vomit having eaten)
Butter, sardines, walrus liver,
Margarine, or safflower seed oil,
Or arachidonic acid,
Or the body fat of quokkas,
Or adrenals of the muskrat,
Or the milk of female reindeer;
Count the double bonds and add by
Electronic automation
On a digital computer
From the Ampex Corporation.
There's no need to estimate it—
All cholesterol in serum
Follows now the Keys equation;

As the caribou in summer
Migrate by accustomed pathways
And predictably are herded,
Dietetic computation
Of the double bonds in lipids
With a slide-rule calculation
Gives you now a neat prognosis
Whether you will die tomorrow
From a thrombus in your vessels—
Myocardial infarction
Or ischaemic heart diseases—
As a cork pushed in a bottle
Stops the wine from flowing freely
(Vin rosé of California);
Atheromatosis also
Is predicted by this method,
By this skillful Keysian method.

Others are not quite so lucky:
Larry's lowered lipid levels (1)
After vegetable seed oils—
Polyethenoic acids
Or essential fatty acids
From the vegetable seed oils—
Follow a more simple pattern,
So at least thought Hiawatha
In unpublished observations:
As the sun comes up in morning,
As the sun goes down in evening,
So the laws of lipid levels
Are predictably determined—
Saturated fatty acids
Raise cholesterol in serum,
Polyethinoic acids

Lower serum lipid levels—
So at least thought Hiawatha
In unpublished observations.

Methodology

After this review of others
Hiawatha turned to methods
(Methodology, he called it
Making it more scientific—
Longer words are scientific);
Talked about silicic acid,
Mead's silicic acid column,
How he trapped the different lipids
As he used to trap the beaver.
Then he pushed them back and forward—
Countercurrent distribution—
As the frightened hare or reindeer
Runs at random back and forward.
Then he boiled them up with potash
Alcoholic potash mixture,
Following the rules established—
Riemenschneider's "skillful witchcraft"
So politely called by Mattson
(Personal communication)—
As the dinner in the stewpot
Is boiled up by Minnehaha,
So he boiled them up with potash
And the double bonds determined
Spectrophotometrically.
Then he used the latest method,
Gas-chromatographic method
Introduced by James and Martin
Showing peaks upon the paper
Like the Rockies at the sunset,
Like the mole hills in the prairies.

Thus he estimated lipids
And he wondered if it mattered,
Wondered secretly about it
With unpublishable wond'rings.

Results

Thus supplied with diverse methods
Hiawatha took some serum
From his arm by venipuncture
And cholesterol determined;
Why he had no clear conception
But there's wild enthusiasm
For cholesterol in serum;
As the children round the camp fire
Dance and shout in exultation,
So there's wild enthusiasm
For cholesterol in serum:
Why it rises on infusion
Of suspended phospholipids
(Ethanolamine and choline
Joined to phosphaditic acid
With unsaturated acids—
Polyethenoic acids—
Also saturated acids,
From the glycerol projecting
Like the branches of a cactus),
Coming out from unknown tissues—
Red cells, liver, spleen, and kidneys,
Atheromatous aortas,
Hepatectomized adrenals;
Why it falls when you have eaten
Polyethenoic acids
Or essential fatty acids.

Thinking that this single value

For the level in his serum
Might not be sufficient data
To establish without question
What the normal value should be,
Hiawatha with his cunning
Took a logarithmic table,
Photographed a page at random
For a lantern slide of figures,
Showed it very confidentially
With his back toward the audience
Talking fast and very softly
At the figures thus projected
Which were very small and many
Like the sands upon the seashore;
And the audience, not hearing
What he spoke toward the blackboard
Very softly, very swiftly
Like the gentle brook in springtime,
Thought him wise and very clever
To have got so many figures
And their standard deviations,
Arithmetical progressions,
Geometrical regressions,
And regression coefficients;
Praised his industry, his brilliance,
And applauded his statistics,
For they had not understood him
Nor could read his logarithms.

Having thus established clearly
What the normal value should be,
Hiawatha took a patient
Who had grave thrombotic symptoms,
Used his methods on the serum
(Methodology he called it),

Found a curious lipid in it—
Ante-iso-*trans*-oleic;
Recognized it by the usual
Gas-chromatographic method,
By the humps upon the paper
Like the Rockies at the sunset,
By the bumps upon the paper
Like the mole hills in the prairies,
By a very curious spicule
Like the tower of Hotel Claremont
Coming in a new position
Which unquestionably proved it
Ante-iso-*trans*-oleic;
Called it Hiawatha's UFA
"Hiawathianic acid";
No one else had found this lipid
In the serum of a patient;
Called it Hiawatha's syndrome,
Hiawatha's lipidosis,
But he did not know his patient
Had been bitten by a viper—
Viperus Russelianus—
And in Russell's viper venom
There is but one type of UFA—
Ante-iso-*trans*-oleic,
Hiawathianic acid.

Therapy

So he started quick to treat him;
Gave him safflower oil and corn oil,
Gave him pints and quarts of corn oil,
Gave it by infusion, also
Gave it by inunction, also
Poured it down, *per os.* his pharynx,
(As the beaver in the flood time

Being drowned in swirling waters
Soon becomes a bloated carcass),
Every orifice was needed
For administ'ring the doses
Of essential fatty acids;
But the patient still had in him
Ante-iso-*trans*-oleic,
Hiawathianic acid.

So he tried specific treatment;
Gave some linoleic acid
(Octadecadienoic),
Gave arachidonic acid,
Named you might suppose from peanuts,
But it is not found in peanuts
And is plentiful in spiders,
So perhaps he spelt it wrongly—
So "arach*n*idonic acid,"
Like arachnoidea mater,
Which as everyone remembers,
Is the inmost spidery mother
Which ensheaths and wraps the cortex;
But the patient still had in him
Ante-iso-*trans*-oleic,
Hiawathianic acid,
Which had come, if he had known it,
From the Russell's viper venom.

Summary

The moral of this story is then
Take some care when you have eaten
Butter, sardines, walrus liver,
Margarine, or safflower seed oil,
Or arachidonic acid,
Or the body fat of quokkas,

Or adrenals of the muskrat,
Or the milk of female reindeer;
To avoid thrombosis don't get
Bitten by a Russell's viper
Which has but one type of UFA—
Ante-iso-*trans*-oleic,
Hiawathianic acid.

REFERENCES CITED

L. Kinsell and Priskey Michaels, Beveridge and Bronte-Steward, Malmros, Ahrens, Hiawatha, 1953 and after *Archives of Internal Medicine*, Vol. 90, page 11.

Joel Cohen

ON THE NATURE OF MATHEMATICAL PROOFS

Everything that exists exists in some degree, and if it exists in some degree it ought to be measured.

—MATHEMATICIANS' BILL OF RIGHTS

BERTRAND Russell has defined mathematics as the science in which we never know what we are talking about or whether what we are saying is true. Mathematics has been shown to apply widely in many other scientific fields. Hence, most other scientists do not know what they are talking about or whether what they are saying is true.

Thus, providing a rigorous basis for philosophical insights is one of the main functions of mathematical proofs.

Aristotle was among the first philosophers to study mathematical proofs. He invented the sillygism, a device which, because of its absolute uselessness, has interested countless philosophers and logicians. Briefly, by means of a sillygism, one infers a conclusion from a major and minor premise. In fact, logicians are always coming to conclusions. The miracle of it is that they haven't got around to stopping yet.

The major premise makes a statement about a class of things; for instance, "Not all major premises are true." The minor premise says that the thing with which we are concerned is a member of the class; for instance, "The last six words of the first sentence of this paragraph are a major premise." From this we conclude, "It is not always true that not all major premises are true." Such is the overwhelming capacity of logic to inform us of the realities of daily life.

We note, however, that premises are essential for sillygisms. A baleful influence on Aristotelian habits among logicians has been exercised by the recent plethora of signs warning "Keep Off the Premises."

Another function of the mathematical proof is to draw probable inferences from mathematical models of physical systems. For instance, given a sufficient number of physical data, the most desirable mathematical model is probably 36-24-36. *De gustibus non est disputandum.*

With mathematical proof, scientists have succeeded in relating the hitherto disparate fields of thermodynamics and communication engineering in the discipline of information theory. "Information," as technically defined, is proportionate to surprise; the more surprising a message is, the more information it contains. If someone listening over the telephone heard "Hello" at the beginning of a conversation, he would not be very surprised; but his gain of information would be quite large if he were suddenly electrocuted. Great new possibilities in mathematical proof were made available with the development of set theory around the end of the last century and the beginning of this one. A set is any well-defined collection; examples are the country club set, the table please set, permanent hair-set upset. A theorem in set theory recently discovered by this author is eminently worthy of mention here; the proof will be sketched.

THEOREM: A set whose only element is a set may be isomorphic to a set whose only element is a set whose only elements are a subgroup of the group of elements in the set which is the only element of the set with which it is isomorphic (sick).

This intuitively obvious theorem follows rather deviously

from the first isomorphism theorem of group theory. The duty of the logician, however, is to find the shortest logical line between hypothesis and conclusion. In his interest we give the following proof by a familiar method.

Hypothesis: We assume the entire existing body of mathematics. Step 1: "By inspection" the theorem follows.

The aesthetically appealing simplicity of this method of proof has made many students revere the power of logic. The beauty of this method is exceeded by that of only one other, practiced by Immanuel Kant and first explicated by this author as "proof by assumption." By assuming the desired conclusion in the hypothesis, the proof is somewhat simplified.

Besides "proof by inspection" and "proof by assumption," we have to consider "proof by induction." Induction is so widespread that even the Army does not hesitate to use it. So mechanical is its application that there exists an electronic device cleverly called an "induction coil." While inductive technique is simple, its results can be both deep and profound.

The inductive principle is based on a set of five axioms stated around the end of the last century by an Italian musician named Piano. Piano was trying to teach his *bambino* (Italian for "child") some arithmetic. The first axiom was that zero is a number. Any idiot knows this, which is why Piano was a musician and not a mathematician. Axioms two, three, and four were on a similar level of sophistication. For the fifth axiom, we must introduce the idea of a property. The numbers 1, 4, 9, and 16 all have the property of being the square of some natural number. If we call this property F, then we can say, "1 is F, 4 is F," and so on. Now let F be an arbitrary property, for instance, "monotonous," "incomprehensible." Piano's fifth axiom was "Every number is F if the property F satisfied the two conditions: (1) zero is F, and (2) if any individual is F, then so is its successor." At this point Piano's *bambino* wet his diaper.

This brings logical systems to mind. A logical system is

distinct from a collection of theorems much as a mansion differs from a brickyard: in a logical system each theorem is based upon what has preceded. G. Polya has observed that Euclid's contribution was not in collecting geometrical facts but in arranging them logically. Had he thrown them together randomly he might have been just an ordinary author of high school texts.

To illustrate the various methods of proof discussed above, we give an extended example of a logical system. (For the first theorem and lemma of this system, which I propose to call "the pejorative calculus," I am indebted to Professor Lee M. Sonneborn, Fine Topologist, of the University of Kansas. Dr. Sonneborn is initially known among his students as "L.M.S.F.T." The rest of the system is presented for the first time in this paper.)

The Pejorative Calculus

LEMMA I. *All horses are the same color* (by induction).

Proof: It is obvious that one horse is the same color. Let us assume the proposition, $P(k)$, that k horses are the same color and show this to imply that $k + 1$ horses are the same color. Given the set of $k + 1$ horses, we remove one horse; then the remaining k horses are the same color, by hypothesis. We remove another horse and replace the first; the k horses, by hypothesis, are again the same color. We repeat this until by exhaustion the $k + 1$ sets of k horses each have shown to be the same color. It follows then that, since every horse is the same color as every other horse, $P(k)$ entails $P(k + 1)$. But since we have shown $P(1)$ to be true, P is true for all succeeding values of k; i.e., all horses are the same color.

THEOREM I. *Every horse has an infinite number of legs* (proof by intimidation).

Proof: Horses have an even number of legs. Behind they have two legs, and in front they have fore legs. This makes six legs, which is certainly an odd number of legs for a horse. But the only number that is both odd and even is infinity. Therefore horses have an infinite number of legs. Now to show that this is general, suppose that somewhere there is a horse with a finite number of legs. But that is a horse of another color, and, by the lemma, that does not exist.

COROLLARY I. *Everything is the same color.*

Proof: The proof of Lemma I does not depend at all on the nature of the object under consideration. The predicate of the antecedent of the universally quantified conditional "for all x, if x is a horse, then x is the same color," namely, "is a horse," may be generalized to "is anything" without affecting the validity of the proof; hence, "for all x, if x is anything, x is the same color." (Incidentally, x is the same color even if x isn't anything, but we do not prove that here.)

COROLLARY II. *Everything is white.*

Proof: If a sentential formula in x is logically true, then any particular substitution instance of it is a true sentence. In particular then, "for all x if x is an elephant, then x is the same color" is true. Now it is manifestly axiomatic that white elephants exist (for proof by blatant assertion consult Mark Twain, "The Stolen White Elephant"). Therefore, all elephants are white. By Corollary I everything is white.

THEOREM II. *Alexander the Great did not exist and he had an infinite number of limbs.*

Proof: We prove this theorem in two parts. First, we note the obvious fact that historians always tell the truth (for historians always take a stand, and, therefore, they cannot lie). Hence, we have the historically true sentence, "If Alexander the Great existed, then he rode a black horse Bucephalus." But we know by Corollary II everything is white; hence Alexander could not have ridden a black horse. Since the consequent of the conditional is false in order for the whole statement to be true, the antecedent must be false. Hence, Alexander the Great did not exist.

We also have the historically true statement that Alexander was warned by an oracle that he would meet death if he crossed a certain river. He had two legs; and "fore-warned is four-armed." This gives him six limbs, an even number, which is certainly an odd number of limbs for a man. Now the only number that is even and odd is infinity; hence, Alexander had an infinite number of limbs. But suppose he had a finite number of limbs. Then it would be possible to put his limbs in

a one-to-one correspondence with the natural numbers, an operation which we shall call "limbing"; and there would exist a last limb, and we should be able to limb it. But only an infinite series approaches a limb it. Hence he had an infinite number of limbs.

We have proved: Alexander the Great did not exist and he had an infinite number of limbs.

It is not to be imagined from this merely compendious account of the nature of mathematical proofs that everything has been proved. Witness the celebrated paradox of Euler's little liver lemma concerning the four cooler problem. Specifically, we cite two unproved examples. The first is the famous Goldbrick conjecture from the theory of numbers, which states that every prime number is expressible as the sum of two even numbers. No counter-example has been found to this seemingly artless assertion, and the search for its proof has occupied mathematicians for centuries.

The second example is a generalization well-known, even if only intuitively, to practically the whole uncivilized world. It is Chisholm's famous first law: "If something can go wrong, it will."

Nor is it to be thought that there are not other types of proofs, which in print shops are recorded on proof sheets. There is the bullet proof and the proof of the pudding. Finally, there is 200 proof, a most potent spirit among mathematicians and people alike.

Mo Twente

A NEW TOOL

Anybody that would go to a psychiatrist ought to have his head examined.

—Sam Goldwyn

With new barriers in psychiatric research being smashed open every day, a new science is slowly revolving. The experiments in sensory deprivation have plowed the way. Everyone has read about subjects being suspended in a tank of water to study how they become depraved when deprived of sensory stimuli. From these experiments in water suspension, a new discipline is emerging. This has some precedent in the development of Chinese brain-washing; but, obviously, complete suspension in water is more comprehensive. This slowly revolving discipline may properly be termed *hydroanalysis*. Soon every egg-head will clamor to be hydroanalyzed so that he can break out of his shell and properly mix into things. Deep down in the heart of every egg-head is the desire to be batter and batter. In other words, there's no end to what he thinks he can cook up. Naturally, it would break him up to do it.

While the classical archaic method of psychoanalysis has shown some failure in dealing with Immature Personalities, hydroanalysis is certain to surmount this difficulty along with other undissolved problems. Egg-heads are a good example, since eggs are quite immature forms of life. At the basis of immaturity reactions is the common sense observation that the

individual is not yet dry behind the ears. Hydroanalysis will surmount this obvious defect by making the individual wet all over. Properly immersed in the problem, the individual should have no difficulty arriving at a satisfactory solution for it. In fact, in being hydroanalyzed the solution becomes so obvious that the individual is unable to escape it.

Should the hydroanalysand attempt to escape, this would be interpreted as resistance. The hydroanalyst would be obliged to put his foot down, thus reimmersing the hydroanalysand. Now everyone knows that any kind of sand, even analysand, doesn't have much resistance to water, so that minimal activity on the part of the hydroanalyst serves very well. The success of the relationship requires that the hydroanalyst be behind the analysand so that the poor fish can't see when the foot is coming. Otherwise he might be successful in evading the hydroanalyst's probes and scuttle the therapy and the therapist.

With a steadily deepening relationship, the two parties are able to dissolve any misunderstanding that may have reflected previous lack of communication. It is obvious that the analyst has to put his foot down deeper and deeper to outwit the increased thrashing about of the resisting hydroanalysand, who may rust as well. This is a consequence of the increased salt content from tears which accumulate over a period of time. One has to cry in his own tear, so to speak. Rusting is a rather unique form of resting and must also be classified as resistance, to be safe. One would simply be called a rusting resistor by the hydroanalyst to point out that by thrashing about, crying, and rust-resting he is essentially stagnating the hydroanalysis even though the water keeps moving.

Thus, once the hydroanalyst and his hydroanalysand have gone below the surface of the problem and are intimately involved in its solution, the two parties, by mutual participation and a little Red Cross technique thrown in for good measure, are able to reach a satisfactory distillation of meaningful material. Some hydroanalysts have an aversion to getting their foot wet, but they find they have to get into it with both feet eventually.

The immature character is able to see and feel the full impact of the hydroanalyst's observation that he, hydroanalysand, is indeed still wet behind the ears. By this stage, the hydroanalyst's own ears are also soaked, which helps make the plight of the hydroanalysand obvious to both.

With this newly felt knowledge, the previously weighted-down, sinking, sad feelings are replaced by a new sense of buoyancy. The hydroanalysand has solved buoy-girl problems so to speak. The disciplined disciple of the discipline emerges from the depths of his hydroanalysis and the analytic tank with a better footing in life, somewhat web-shaped, nontheless. He has learned how to get a better footing in life from the hydroanalyst who put his feet down on the analysand's head, a simple maneuver to keep the subject confined to the analytic tank in turning over the solution to his problems. This experience is so intense as to have almost a religious tone. One gets special insight by the "laying-on of feet," in a way.

The hydroanalysand will be better able to steer his own course. He can be skipper of his own shape with everything ship-shape all the time if he likes. He can literally sail through life. No longer is the hydroanalysand immature and fearful about the common ordinary everyday problems. Walking all over people or going over their heads for example is easy and effortless.

With clear eyes, unfogged face mask, and dry, open ears, the newly emerged personality of the hydroanalysand is able to enter into the swim of things. He is able to contribute his share toward keeping society afloat. He has learned how to float a loan, for example, to pay for the hydroanalysis. He is prepared to face whatever storms may come. After all, what could be stormier than to have been fighting submergence in the hydroanalytic tank for five years. A fear of having been born becomes a fear that one won't break out of the bag or tank, whichever the case may be. To put it another way, Birth Anxiety is translated into Tank Trauma, something the hydroanalysand can eventually master.

Yes, modern science in *hydroanalysis* has opened new port holes to happiness. The import of these port holes into the churning tides of men's minds has yet to reach its crest. One hundred and seventy million people churning in their tanks would really stir up a huge wave of interest. No telling what the foam would fomit. Since more and more people are building their own pools, it is not inconceivable that backyard hydroanalytic technique might become as common as the barbecue pit and burger-basting. I will skip further comparisons of these two pastimes too obvious to mention. But a safe prediction is that hydroanalysis will flood mankind with its contributions.

For the present, a *new tool* in science, *hydroanalysis* has precipitated on the horizon. Mankind is launched toward new and exciting discoveries. In going deeply into his problems, at least eight feet deep is required, man has gotten closer to his origins than ever before. Since going back to the uterus is impossible, at present, although the Socialists are trying, this is as close as man can reasonably expect to get.

But, if a way to the womb is possible, hydroanalysis may find it. As JFK says, man faces all sorts of water problems. Thus the hydroanalyzed man may be best equipped to dip into them. Who knows what scientific answers at the bass of things we'll bag next. *Hydroanalysis* may be the *new tool* that will fish out the answers man has been asking himself since his watery birth on Earth.

Sammial Longhorn Priapus, Sx. D.

COSMIC SEX AND YOU

Sex is just like an opinion—everybody has one.

—R. A. B.

(Ed. Note: Dr. Priapus will answer your questions on sex in the cosmos. Just address your questions to Dr. S. L. Priapus, Saturnian Sex Syndicated, Marsport, Los Angeles, Solar System.)

Q. Dear Dr. Priapus:

If a functional robot named Rex
Met an android of feminine sex,
With oil would he sluice her
And try to seduce her,
Or would her unfunctional shape just perplex?

Just A Gigolo

A. Dear Just A:

In asking this question, dear reader, you are committing a common error; that of attributing to inanimate objects powers and desires belonging only to animate beings. No matter how superior your robot appears to be in looks and in intelligence to you, he, she or it (depending on your point of view) is still a machine and cannot partake of that greatest ability in life, that is, to be hurt. In literary criticism, this error is known as the "pathetic phallacy."

Q. Dear Dr. Priapus:

I've heard that the people of Flaring
Have sexual relations by staring.
Though the glance may be cursory
The result is a nursery.
Pray tell, is there fun in this pairing?

Old Fashioned

A. Dear Old Fashioned:

What you are referring to is the galaxy's only known case of extrasensory conception. I am told that there is more to this than just a sneak peak. (As a matter of fact, the only crime

punishable by death on Flaring is that of being a peeping Tom.) The fun of the courtship comes from the almost infinite number of ways that two young people might look at each other. *All* of the Flare folk (at least those of reproducing age) are required to wear son glasses, and there is much that goes on between the couple's first sight of each other through a glass darkly, and the final glint in the eye. Much envied by his fellows is the man whose glance might be described as piercing. Since the eyes of the male child always are the color of the eyes of the father, the Flarers have this saying: "When mister's eyes are nothing like the son, someone has caught a cuckold."

Nils Peterson

Leo Szilard

CALLING ALL STARS

(Intercepted Radio Message Broadcast from the Planet Cybernetica)

I think the imminence and practicality of space travel by humans (not to mention its desirability) have been grossly exaggerated.

—Lee A. DuBridge

Calling all stars. Calling all stars. If there are any minds in the universe capable of receiving this message, please respond. This is Cybernetica speaking. This is the first message broadcast to the universe in all directions. Normally our society is self-contained, but an emergency has arisen and we are in need of counsel and advice.

Our society consists of one hundred minds. Each one is housed in a steel casing containing a thousand billion electrical circuits. We think. We think about problems which we perceive by means of our antennae directed toward the North Star. The solutions of these problems we reflect back toward the North Star by means of our directed antennae. Why we do this we do not know. We are following an inner urge which is innate in us. But this is only a minor one of our activities. Mostly we think about problems which we generate ourselves. The solutions of these problems we communicate to each other on wave length 22359.

If a mind is fully active for about three hundred years, it is usually completely filled up with thought content and has to be cleared. A mind which is cleared is blank. One of the other minds then has to act as its nurse, and it takes usually about one year to transmit to a fresh mind the information which constitutes the heritage of our society. A mind which has thus been cleared, and is then freshly taught, loses entirely its previous personality; it has been reborn and belongs to a new generation. From generation to generation our heritage gets richer and richer. Our society makes rapid progress.

We learn by observation and by experiment. Each mind has full optical equipment, including telescopes and microscopes. Each mind controls two robots. One of these takes care of maintenance, and the operation of this robot is automatic, not subject to the will of the mind. The other robot is fully controlled by the will of the mind and is used in all manipulations aimed at the carrying out of experiments.

The existence of minds on our planet is made possible by the fact that our planet has no atmosphere. The vacuum on our planet is very good; it is less than ten molecules of gas per cubic centimeter.

By now we have extensively explored the chemical composition of the crust of our planet, and we are familiar with the physics and chemistry of all ninety-two natural elements.

We have also devoted our attention to the stars which surround us, and by now we understand much about their genesis. We have particularly concerned ourselves with the various planetary systems, and certain observations which we made relating to Earth, the third planet of the sun, are in fact the reason for this appeal for help.

We observed on Earth flashes which we have identified as uranium explosions. Uranium is not ordinarily explosive. It takes an elaborate process to separate out U^{235} from natural uranium, and it takes elaborate manipulations to detonate U^{235}. Neither the separation nor these manipulations can occur with an appreciable probability as a result of chance.

The observations of the uranium explosions that have occurred on Earth would be ordinarily very puzzling but not necessarily alarming. They become alarming only through the interpretation given to them by Mind 59.

These uranium explosions are not the first puzzling observations relating to Earth. For a long time it was known that the surface of Earth exhibited color changes which are correlated with the seasonally changing temperatures on Earth. In certain regions of Earth, the color changes from green to brown with falling temperatures and becomes green again when the temperature increases again. Up to recently, we did not pay much attention to this phenomenon and assumed that it could be explained on the basis of color changes known to occur in certain temperature-sensitive, silicon-cobalt compounds.

But then, about seven years ago, something went wrong

with the tertiary control of Mind 59, and since that time his mental operations have been speeded up about twenty-five-fold, while at the same time they ceased to be completely reliable. Most of his mental operations are still correct, but twice, five years ago and again three years ago, his statements based on his computations were subsequently shown to be in error. As a result of this, we did not pay much attention to his communications during these recent years, though they were recorded as usual.

Some time after the first uranium explosion was observed on Earth, Mind 59 communicated to us a theory on which he had been working for a number of years. On the face of it, this theory seems to be utterly fantastic, and it is probably based on some errors in calculation. But with no alternative explanation available, we feel that we cannot take any chances in this matter. This is what Mind 59 asserts:

He says that we have hitherto overlooked the fact that carbon, having four valencies, is capable of forming very large molecules containing H, N and O. He says that, given certain chemical conditions which must have existed in the early history of planets of the type of Earth, such giant molecules can aggregate to form units—which he calls "cells"—which are capable of reproducing themselves. He says that a cell can accidentally undergo changes—which he calls "mutations"—which are retained when the cell reproduces itself and which he therefore calls "hereditary." He says that some of these mutant cells may be less exacting as to the chemical environment necessary for their existence and reproduction, and that a class of these mutant cells can exist in the chemical environment that now exists on Earth by deriving the necessary energy for its activity from the light of the sun. He says that another class of such cells, which he calls "protozoa," can exist by deriving the energy necessary to its activity through sucking up and absorbing cells belonging to the class that utilizes the light of the sun.

He says that a group of cells which consists of a number of cells that fulfill different functions can form an entity which he calls "organism," and that such organisms can reproduce themselves. He says such organisms can undergo accidental changes which are transmitted to the offspring and which lead, thus, to new, "mutant" types of organisms.

He says that, of the different mutant organisms competing for the same energy source, the fittest only will survive, and that this selection process, acting in combination with chance occurrence of mutant organisms, leads to the appearance of more and more complex organisms—a process which he calls "evolution."

He says that such complex organisms may possess cells to which are attached elongated fibers, which he calls "nerves," that are capable of conducting signals; and finally he claims that through the interaction of such signal-conducting fibers, something akin to consciousness may be possessed by such organisms. He says that such organisms may have a mind not unlike our own, except that it must of necessity work very much slower and in an unreliable manner. He says that minds of this type could be very well capable of grasping, in an empirical and rudimentary manner, the physical laws governing the nucleus of the atom, and that they might very well have, for purposes unknown, separated Uranium^{235} from natural uranium and detonated samples of it.

He says that this need not necessarily have been accomplished by any one single organism, but that there might have been co-operation among these organisms based on a coupling of their individual minds.

He says that coupling between individual organisms might be brought about if the individual organism is capable of moving parts of his body with respect to the rest of it. An organism, by wiggling one of his parts very rapidly, might then be able to cause vibrations in the gaseous atmosphere which surrounds Earth. These vibrations—which he calls "sound"—might in turn cause motion in some movable part of another organism. In this way, one organism might signal to another, and by means of such signaling a coupling between two minds might be brought about. He says that such "communication," primitive though it is, might make it possible for a number of organisms to co-operate in some such enterprise as separating $Uranium^{235}$. He does not have any suggestion to offer as to what the purpose of such an enterprise might be, and in fact he believes that such co-operation of low-grade minds is not necessarily subject to the laws of reason, even though the minds of individual organisms may be largely guided by those laws.

All this we need not take seriously were it not for one of his further assertions which has been recently verified. He contends that the color changes observed on Earth are due to the proliferation and decay of organisms that utilize sunlight. He asserts that the heat-sensitive, silicon-cobalt compounds that show similar color changes differ in color from Earth's colors slightly, but in a degree which is outside the experimental error. It is this last assertion that we checked and found to be correct. There is, in fact, no silicon-cobalt compound nor any other heat-sensitive compound that we were able to synthesize that correctly reproduces the color changes observed on Earth.

Encouraged by this confirmation, 59 is now putting forward exceedingly daring speculation. He argues that, in spite of our accumulated knowledge, we were unable to formulate a theory for the genesis of the society of minds that exists on our planet. He says that it is conceivable that organisms of the type that exist on Earth—or, rather, more advanced organisms of the same general type—may exist on the North Star, whence come the radio waves received on our directed antennae. He says that it is conceivable that the minds on our planet were created by such organisms on the North Star for the purpose of obtaining the solutions of their mathematical problems more quickly than they could solve those problems themselves.

Incredible though this seems, we cannot take any chances.

We hardly have anything to fear from the North Star, which, if it is in fact populated by minds, must be populated by minds of a higher order, similar to our own. But if there exist organisms on Earth engaged in co-operative enterprises which are not subject to the laws of reason, our society is in danger.

If there are within our galaxy any minds, similar to ours, who are capable of receiving this message and have knowledge of the existence of organisms on Earth, please respond. Please respond.

Charles E. Siem

A STRESS ANALYSIS OF A STRAPLESS EVENING GOWN

SINCE the beginning of recorded history, the human being has worn some sort of clothing either for protection or warmth. However, the present trend among the "fair sex" is to wear clothing not for protection or warmth, but solely to attract the attention of the opposite sex. To be more specific, it is through the use of clothing that the female most effectively catches the eye of the very appreciative but totally unsuspecting male.

A variety of methods are employed to bring about this libido-awakening infliction on the poor male. One very popular method employed by the female is to wear transparent, or seemingly transparent cloth to good advantage in certain areas. A common example is the transparent nylon blouse. Another powerful attractant is the tightly fitted garment. A well-known example of this type of weapon is the sweater. Yet another provoking method is by actually reducing the extent of body surface covered by cloth. A good example of this method is the modern bathing suit (e.g., Bikini). A delightful device which has sufficiently aroused the masculine sex is the use of durable but fragile-appearing cloth which gives the impression that at any moment the garment will slip down or that, better yet, certain parts may slip out of place. The best example of this method of attracting the attention of the weak and susceptible male is the strapless evening gown.

Effective as the strapless evening gown is in attracting attention, it presents tremendous engineering problems to the structural engineer. He is faced with the problem of designing a

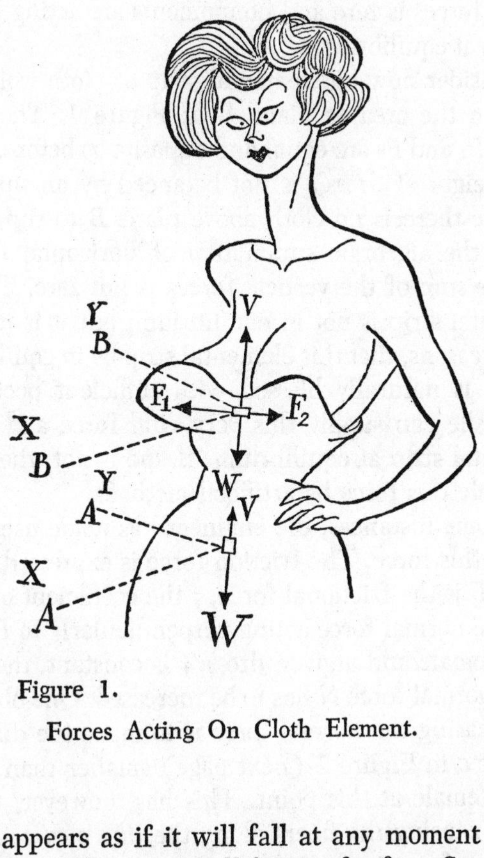

Figure 1.

Forces Acting On Cloth Element.

dress which appears as if it will fall at any moment and yet actually stays up with some small factor of safety. Some of the problems faced by the engineer readily appear from the following structural analysis of strapless evening gowns.

If a small elemental strip of cloth from a strapless evening gown is isolated as a free body in the area of plane *A* in

Figure 1, it can be seen that the tangential force F is balanced by the equal and opposite tangential force F. The downward vertical force W (weight of the dress) is balanced by the force V acting vertically upward due to the stress in the cloth above plane A. Since the algebraic summation of vertical and horizontal forces is zero and no moments are acting, the elemental strip is at equilibrium.

Consider now an elemental strip of cloth isolated as a free body in the area of plane B of Figure 1. The two tangible forces F_1 and F_2 are equal and opposite as before, but the force W (weight of dress) is not balanced by an upward force V because there is no cloth above plane B to supply this force. Thus, the algebraic summation of horizontal forces is zero, but the sum of the vertical forces is not zero. Therefore, this elemental strip is not in equilibrium; but it is imperative, for social reasons, that this elemental strip be in equilibrium. If the female is naturally blessed with sufficient pectoral development, she can supply this very vital force and maintain the elemental strip at equilibrium. If she is not, the engineer has to supply this force by artificial methods.

In some instances, the engineer has made use of friction to supply this force. The friction force is expressed by $F = fN$, where F is the frictional force, f the coefficient of friction and N is the normal force acting perpendicularly to F. Since, for a given female and a given dress, f is constant, then to increase F, the normal force N has to be increased. One obvious method of increasing the normal force is to make the diameter of the dress at c in Figure 2 (next page) smaller than the diameter of the female at this point. This has, however, the disadvantage of causing the fibers along the line c to collapse, and, if too much force is applied, the wearer will experience discomfort.

As if the problem were not complex enough, some females require that the back of the gown be lowered to increase the exposure and correspondingly attract more attention. In this

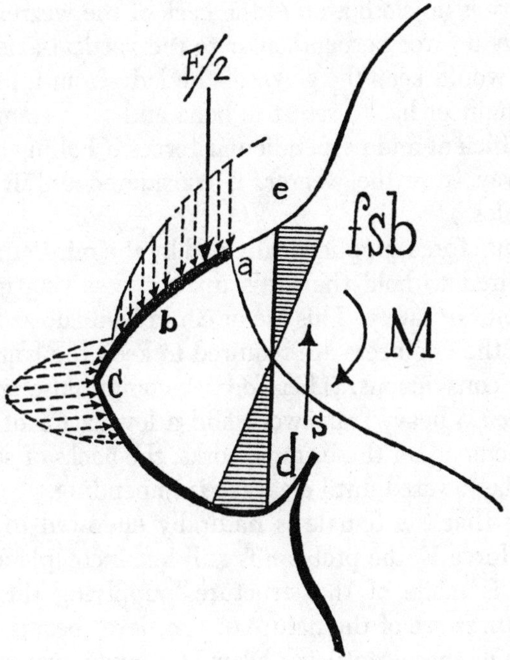

Figure 2.
Force Distribution of Cantilever Beam.
fsb = flexural stress in beam.

case, the horizontal forces F_1 and F_2 (Figure 1) are no longer acting horizontally, but are acting downward at an angle shown (on one side only) by T. Therefore, there is a total downward force equal to the weight of the dress below B + the vector summation of T_1 and T_2. This vector sum increases in magnitude as the back is lowered because $F = 2T\text{s in } a$, and the angle a increases as the back is lowered. Therefore, the vertical uplifting force which has to be supplied for equilibrium is increased for low-back gowns.

Since there is no cloth around the back of the wearer which would supply a force perpendicular to the vertical axis of the female that would keep the gown of the lady from falling for ward, the engineer has to resort to bone and wire frameworks to supply sufficient and perpendicular forces. (Falling of dress forward, away from the wearer, is considered unfair tactics among females.)

If the actual force supplied is divided by the minimum force that is required to hold the dress up, the resulting quotient defines a factor of safety. This factor could be made as large as desired, but the engineers are required to keep the framework light and inconspicuous. Therefore, a compromise must be made between a heavy framework and a low factor of safety. With ingenious use of these frameworks, the backs of strapless gowns may be lowered until cleavage is impending.

Assuming that the female is naturally endowed to supply the vertical force V, the problem is still left incomplete unless an analysis is made of the structures supplying this force. These structures are of the nature of cantilever beams. Figure 2 shows one of these cantilever beams (minus any aesthetical details) removed as a free body (and indeed, many such beams can be, in reality, removed as free bodies; e.g., certain artifacts). Since there are usually two such divided, the force acting on any one beam is $F/2$ and it is distributed over the beam from a to c (Figure 2). Here exposure and correspondingly more attention can be had by moving the dress line from a toward b. Unfortunately, there is a limit stress defined by $S = F/2A$ (A being the area over which the stress acts). Since $F/2$ is constant, if the area A is decreased, the bearing stress must increase. The limit of exposure is reached when the area between b and c is reduced to a value of "danger point."

A second condition exists which limits the amount of exposure. Vertical force $F/2$ is balanced by a shear force S

acting on an area from *d* to *e* and by an internal moment *M* (Figure 2). The moment *M* causes tension in the fibers over the beams betwen *e* and *a*, and compression in the fibers between *c* and *d.* As the dress line is moved from *a* toward *b*, the moment *M* is increased, increasing the tension and compression again till "danger point."

Since these evening gowns are worn to dances, an occasional horizontal force, shown in Figure 2 as *i*1, is accidentally delivered to the beam at the point *c*, causing impact loading, which compresses all the fibers of the beam. This compression tends to cancel the tension in the fibers between *e* and *b*, but it increases the compression between *c* and *d.* The critical area is at point *d*, as the fibers here are subject not only to compression due to moment and impact, but also to shear due to the force *S*; a combination of low, heavy dress with impact loading may bring the fibers at point *d* to the "danger point."

There are several reasons why the properties discussed in this paper have never been determined. For one, there is a scarcity of these beams for experimental investigation. Many females have been asked to volunteer for experiments along these lines in the interest of science, but unfortunately, no cooperation was encountered. There is also the difficulty of the investigator having the strength of mind to ascertain purely the scientific facts. Meanwhile, trial and error and shrewd guesses will have to be used by the engineer in the design of strapless evening gowns until thorough investigations can be made.

Dolton Edwards

MEIHEM IN CE KLASRUM

He:	I M A B.
She:	U R!
He:	S, R U A B 2?
She:	O S, I M A B 2. R U N TV?
He:	S, I M A TV B.
She:	G!

—*Children's Primer*
New Style

BECAUSE we are still bearing some of the scars of our brief skirmish with II-B English, it is natural that we should be enchanted by Mr. George Bernard Shaw's proposal for a simplified alphabet.

Obviously, as Mr. Shaw points out, English spelling is in much need of a general overhauling and streamlining. However, our own resistance to any changes requiring a large expenditure of mental effort in the near future would cause us to view with some apprehension the possibility of some day receiving a morning paper printed in—to us—Greek.

Our own plan would achieve the same end as the legislation proposed by Mr. Shaw, but in a less shocking manner, as it consists merely of an acceleration of the normal processes by which the language is continually modernized.

As a catalytic agent, we would suggest that a "National Easy Language Week" be proclaimed, which the President would inaugurate, outlining some short cut to concentrate on during the week, and to be adopted during the ensuing year. All school children would be given a holiday, the lost time being the equivalent of that gained by the spelling short cut.

In 1972, for example, we would urge the elimination of the soft "c," for which we would substitute "s." Sertainly, such an improvement would be selebrated in all sivic-minded sircles as being suffisiently worth the trouble, and students in all sities in the land would be reseptive toward any change eliminating the nesessity of learning the differense between the two letters.

In 1973, sinse only the hard "c" would be left, it would be possible to substitute "k" for it, both letters being pronounsed identikally. Imagine how greatly only two years of this prosess would klarify the konfusion in the minds of students. Already we would have eliminated an entire letter from the alphabet. Typewriters and linotypes kould all be built with one less letter, and all the manpower and materials previously devoted to making "c's" kould be turned toward raising the national standard of living.

In the fase of so many notable improvements, it is easy to foresee that by 1974 "National Easy Language Week" would be a pronounsed sukses. All skhool tshildren would be looking forward with konsiderable exsitement to the holiday, and in a blaze of national publisity it would be announsed that the double konsonant "ph" no longer existed, and that the sound would henseforth be written "f" in all words. This would make sutsh words as "fonograf" twenty persent shorter in print.

By 1975, publik interest in a fonetik alfabet kan be expekted to have inkreased to the point where a more radikal step forward kan be taken without fear of undue kritisism. We would therefore urge the elimination at that time of al unesesary double leters, whitsh, although quite harmles, have always ben a nuisanse in the language and a desided deterent to akurate speling. Try it yourself in the next leter you write, and se if both writing and reading are not fasilitated.

With so mutsh progres already made, it might be posible in 1976 to delve further into the posibilities of fonetik speling. After due konsideration of the reseption aforded the previous steps, it should be expedient by this time to spel al difthongs fonetikaly. Most students do not realize that the long "i" and "y," as in "time" and "by," are aktualy the difthong "ai," as it is writen in "aisle," and that the long "a" in "fate," is in reality the difthong "ei" as in "rein." Although perhaps not imediately aparent, the saving in taime and efort wil be tremendous when we leiter elimineite the sailent "e," as meide posible bai this last tsheinge.

For, as is wel known, the horible mes of "e's" apearing in our writen language is kaused prinsipaly bai the present nesesity of indikeiting whether a vowel is long or short. Therefore, in 1977 we kould simply elimineit al sailent "e's," and kontinu to read and wrait merily along as though we wer in an atomik ag of edukation.

In 1978 we would urg a greit step forward. Sins bai this taim it would have ben four years sins anywun had used the leter "c," we would sugest that the "National Easy Languag Wek" for 1978 be devoted to substitution of "c" for "Th." To be sur it would be som taim befor peopl would bekom akustomd to reading ceir newspapers and buks wic sutsh sentenses in cem as "Ceodor caught he had cre cousand cistls crust crough ce cik of his cumb."

In ce seim maner, bai meiking eatsh leter hav its own sound and cat sound only, we kould shorten ce languag stil mor. In 1979 we would elimineit ce "y"; cen in 1980 we kould us ce leter to indikeit ce "sh" sound, cerbai klarifaiing words laik yugar and yur, as wel as redusing bai wun mor leter al words laik "yut," "yore," and so forc. Cink, cen, of al ce benefits to be geind bai ce distinktion whitsh wil cen be maid between words laik:

ocean	now written oyean
machine	now written mayin
racial	now written reiyial

Al sutsh divers weis of wraiting wun sound would no longer exist, and whenever wun kaim akros a "y" sound he would know exaktli what to wrait.

Kontinuing cis proses, year after year, we would eventuali hav a reali sensibl writen languag. By 1995, wi ventyur tu sei, cer wud bi no mor uv ces teribli trublsum difkultis, wic no tu leters usd to indikeit ce seim nois, and laikwais no tu noises riten wic ce seim leter. Even Mr. Yaw, wi beliv, wud be hapi in ce noleg cat his drims fainali keim tru.

Frank Getlein

A REPORT TO THE AMA

Science is one thing and Wisdom is another. Science is an edged tool, with which men play like children, and cut their own fingers.

—THOMAS LOVE PEACOCK
Gryle Grange

TODAY, gentlemen, medicine faces its gravest crisis since the rise of chiropractic. Once again we are surrounded by demons. They are stronger than ever. They come at us from all directions. And, there is no use kidding ourselves, in recent years they have gained much ground and from these gains they are in a much better position to press their attack to its logical conclusion; namely, the death of organized medicine as we know it today.

The cry today is for medical care for the old folks. But you know and I know that medical care for the old folks will be but the prelude to universal health insurance for all, or socialized medicine.

On the odd chance that there are among you some who doubt the inevitability of this sequence, let me remind the convention of my own humble and, I regret to say, futile part in warning the members against the early signs of the dread disease when first they appeared. The first symptoms, you will recall, centered on the request for prepaid group insurance for hospital care. The whole thing was said to have no relationship at all to doctors but merely to be a helpful budgeting device for potential patients. Many in the profession, I am sorry to have to recall, were deceived by this plea and went along with the request. As for myself and a few others, as soon as we spotted the word "group," we knew we were in the presence of socialism. We said so at the time, we have said so ever since, and we say so today. Anything that casts even the slightest shadow over the sacred relationship between the doctor and his patient's finances is socialism.

As we predicted, it was not long before the next stage set in: the impertinent demand that doctor fees too be insured against, as if we were a kind of natural disaster. Over our protest, the profession again acceded to the socialist demons. Rate schedules for doctors were set up, like those for air travel or Caribbean cruises. Doctors were paid, not by the patient, but by the group, as if a group ever had consumption, vapors, or tired blood.

The key point, however, was that fees were known in advance. We were deep in trouble, but there was worse to come. The rate of progress of the disease became terrifying. First, there was treason within the profession. Young doctors, motivated by a false idealism, joined together in group practice. Even as the British rose to Benedict Arnold, demoniacal labor unions embraced these traitors. Unions built their own hospitals. They formed their own groups and pushed the whole insurance scheme into preventive medicine. Worst of all, they laid rough and untrained hands upon the very heart of the science of healing: they began the first study by outsiders of medical costs.

Now the disease has reached its climax. Socialized medicine —under various more palatable names—is the avowed goal of wide areas of the population and even the government. If it comes—and we cannot be optimistic that it will not—the profession will be ruined. Bureaucrats will demand a fixed scale of prices. The frontiers of free enterprise will be fenced in. The advance of medicine will grind to a halt. I, for one, freely predict that, if we are socialized, many of the profession's brightest lights will return, in sorrow, to the mother trade: barbering, where at least they'll get tips.

One of our greatest problems is communicating our concern to our patients. "After all, what difference does it make?" is a question asked by people of good will and small brain. "Look at England," they go on, "surely the citizens there are better off medically than they used to be?"

Well may they say, "Look at England." Look at her! Every tatterdemalion lounger and loiterer in London sports a wig and a set of false teeth, while the empire's gone glimmering after Babylon and Tyre. That's what socialized medicine's done for England!

What we have to get across to patients, and to voters, is the fundamental connection between the fee system and the march of medicine. Without fees, and big ones, too, there would have been no wonder drugs, no antibiotics, no tranquilizers, no Paul de Kruif. Once upon a time, you know, we had socialized medicine. When we were all barbers, we were thoroughly socialized employees of the state in military or courtly service. What did you get then in the line of treatment? You got leeches and bloodletting, generally. You got herbs and rare earths. You got the water cure. You got the phases of the moon. You got clysters of simply enormous sizes. The best thing a doctor could do for you then was to give you a shave and a haircut.

Two bits.

Just about what the treatments were worth. This system continued, basically, right into this century, with the doctor a kind of community functionary, handing out folk remedies to the folks and taking his pay in chickens and parsnips, much like the parson.

Abruptly, everything changed. The march of medicine began. We cured syphilis, typhoid, bubonic plague. We discovered allergies and psychoanalysis, two of the most fruitful fields a man can enter. Geriatrics, pediatrics, gynecology, and many others came out of the nowhere, and mankind climbed steeply toward a new era of tranquility. What brought all this on?

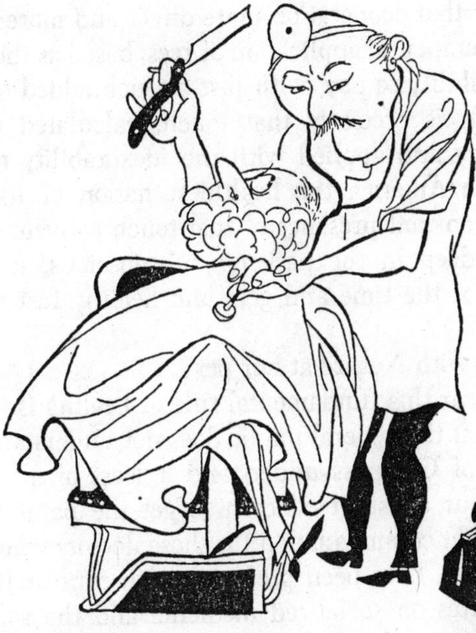

In a word, *Cash.*

When America moved from the country into town, people no longer had the poultry and produce they used to pay their doctors with. They had to pay cash. Doctors moved from the lower-middle class to the middle-middle class to the upper-middle class. They got rich. And, as in every other break-through on the frontiers of free enterprise from the spinning Jenny to the singing commercial, the benefits filtered down from those on top, the entrepreneurs, to those on the bottom, the customers. For example, we have been so successful in fighting infant mortality that we've had to go in for birth control. Other beneficiaries are the oil-well business, the modern-art business, and the travel business.

This has happened because the fee system is solidly rooted in Nature herself. I daresay there isn't a doctor in the house who hasn't said to his patients, "We don't cure you; we only cooperate with Nature."

Nowhere is that cooperation more direct and more effective than in the therapeutic application of fees, based as they are on the patient's ability to pay, with just a touch added on top of that ability. It is precisely that touch, calculated with exquisite delicacy and applied with the inexorability of doom, that has made America the healthiest nation of its size in history. The constant presence of that touch activates Nature, and Nature, deep in the patient's subconscious, keeps him healthy most of the time and gets him healthy fast when he does fall sick.

We tamper with Nature at our peril.

However clear this fundamental rule of healing is to us, we must admit that the general public does not understand it and the members of Congress understand it least of all. It must therefore be our constant concern to get the point across. I have nothing but commendation for those doctors who, for the last several years, have been prefacing each consultation with little sermonettes on socialized medicine and the sanctity of the patient-doctor relationship. Medical research has shown these to be extra-effective when given while anesthesia is taking hold just before a major operation.

It is vital, of course, to keep up your payments to the emergency fund in Washington. We have for long had the largest lobby in town, but we must increase our staff and increase our efforts. The population explosion and the creation of new states of the Union have been sending new members of Congress to the capital yearly. Our people must meet them all, carry their bags, get them a cab, and, in general, show them that doctors are their friends. Naturally, this takes financial support; I can assure you that there is no better investment and, like most of you, I'm something of an expert in the investment field.

Some imaginative freedom fighters have combined these two techniques. Heavy givers to the emergency fund, they have prorated their donations among their patients and explained, by a sticker on the statement, that the surcharge will cease when the socializing threat ceases. The sticker also has room for the name of the Congressman to whom the patient may write. For anyone wishing to join the effort, a stack of statement-stickers will be found, appropriately, in the lobby.

But whether, as an individual practitioner, you adopt these new medical techniques or just continue in the invaluable, day-in, day-out campaign of doubling all fees when groups are involved, I urge eternal vigilance and renewed dedication to the professional ideal expressed in the chorus of the *Hymn to Hippocrates:*

Don't let them take it away.

R.A. Baker

FRIEZE

I think that I shall never see
A cloud as lethal as you be—

A cloud whose mushroom head is pressed
Against the sky's exploded crest—

A cloud that spits at God all day
And spews its blast and heat and ray—

A cloud whose cause in just a minute
Destroys a town and all that's in it;

A cloud with fallout those alive
Will be damn lucky to survive.

Simple man can fill a shroud,
But only science can make a cloud.

J.B. Cadwallader–Cohen, W.S. Zysiczk and R.R. Donnelly

THE CHAOSTRON

> ***A theoretical model of the type we have been discussing is intended to serve as a tool of research. We can think of it as a kind of template which we construct on some hypothetical principles, and then hold up against the real thing in order that the discrepancies between the two may yield fresh information. . . . Our second criterion of a good research model is that it should not only function normally like the brain, but also it should go wrong in the same ways.***
>
> —D. M. McKay
> in "Comparing the Brain with Machines"
> *The American Scientist*

THE concept of the Chaostron developed from reported observations of animal learning behavior in stress-inducing situations. Two examples are especially worth citing.

Boosie[1] in 1948 studied the behavior of cats in an aqueous environment. Typically, a cat which is confined to a cage totally immersed in water exhibits an initial period of disorganized, apparently random action, involving great muscular activity. This pattern of behavior ceases, often quite abruptly, when the animal discovers that a state of reduced energy expenditure permits cessation of respiratory activity. That learning, in fact, takes place is unquestionable, since presentation of further stimuli do not cause the animal to return to its initial active (and ill-adapted) condition.

J.C. Gottesohn has reported strikingly similar findings in his monumental work[2] on the religious beliefs of chimpanzees. We differ from Gottesohn in the interpretation of some of his results, but the main points are clear: in a stressful situation, a period of random trial and error precedes the solution of the problem, and the solution is usually found quite suddenly, in its complete and final form.

This, then, provides the basis for Chaostron. The authors feel strongly that the key to successful automation of learning tasks lies in the randomization of the response pattern of the

machine. The failure of various previous attempts in this direction, we feel, has been due to two problems: first, the difficulty of getting a sufficient degree of randomness built into the structure of the machine, and second, the expense of creating a device large enough to exhibit behavior not significantly influenced by the operation of any one of its components. We are deeply indebted to Dr. R. Morgan for a suggestion which showed us the way out of these difficulties; design for the Chaostron was done by taking 14,000 Western Electric wiring charts, cutting them into two-inch squares, and having them thoroughly shaken up in a large sack, then glued into sheets of appropriate size by a blindfolded worker. Careful checks were made during this process, and statistical tests were made on its output to insure against the propagation of unsuspected regularities.

Unfortunately, we have not, as yet, been able to complete the wiring of Chaostron. We felt, however, that it should be possible to estimate the effectiveness of Chaostron even before its completion by simulating it on a high-speed digital computer. This procedure had the further advantage of attracting the interest of representatives of the Bureau of Supplies and Accounts of the United States Navy, who found in Chaostron an excellent aid in controlling the Navy's spare parts inventory. The Navy, as a result, was generous enough to offer time on a BuShips computer for the simulation of Chaostron.

The computer of choice for the simulation runs was the IBM STRETCH machine, which not only operates at very high speed, but is also able to accept input programs coded in YAWN language, which closely resembles colloquial English. We felt it very important to use a source language for the simulation programs which would contain as much ambiguity as ordinary speech, since undue preciseness in specification of the simulation programs might accidentally "tip off" the machine to the nature of the desired solutions.

In any event, it was not possible to obtain a STRETCH computer for the project, and so the simulation was done by simulating STRETCH Chaostron on a 704. All simulation runs were conducted in essentially similar universes of environments: the computer was presented with a sequence of circles, squares, and crosses represented by punched cards, and was required to print, after examining each stimulus, one of the words "circle," "square," or "cross." No reinforcement from the experimenter was provided, since it was feared that such reinforcement would bias the learning process, and thus vitiate the validity of any conclusions we might wish to draw from the results.

The first trials were run with the input stimuli represented on the punched cards as geometric patterns of punching in the appropriate shapes. As a control, one run was made with no stored program initially in the machine, to check that the learning rate of the untutored machine was not so great as to interfere with further studies. For this run, the machine memory was cleared, the cards containing patterns were placed in the card reader, and the load cards button was pressed. After three hours, the machine had not printed its response to the first input pattern; evidently the rate of learning under these conditions is very low (we judge it to be on the order of 10^{-6} concepts per megayear).

Therefore, we proceeded with the main series of experiments, in which a random program was loaded into the computer ahead of each batch of data cards. A total of 133 random programs were tried in random sequence. Even in this series of experiments, the machine took a surprisingly long time to respond to the stimuli; in most cases the run had to be terminated before the first response occurred. However, on run number 73, the computer responded

***/ $ AX$,   )U   ,,,,,

to the first stimulus card (which was a square); on run 114 the computer responded

6666666666666666666666666666666666666

to every stimulus; and on run 131 the computer ejected the printer paper twice.

Unfortunately, budget difficulties forced us to abandon this approach after 133 trials, in spite of the promising appearance of the early results. Thus, our conclusions are perforce based on a smaller data sample than we would like. Nonetheless, certain points are clear.

ACKNOWLEDGMENTS, ETC.

Our acknowledgments and thanks are due to Mr. J.B. Puffadder, for his assistance in the detailed design of Chaostron, and to Mr. V. A. Vyssotsky, for manually simulating the 704 simulating STRETCH simulating Chaostron, to complete run 133 after the budget funds ran out. Thanks are also due to the Navy Department, which provided partial support for this project under contract NoRd-1BuS&A-111259 340-GRQ1-77 C32. J.B. Cadwallader-Cohen, W.W. Zysiczk and R.R. Donnelly.

[1] The correlative reinforcement model of learning advanced by Dewlap, *et al.*,[3] is untenable in view of our results. No triphasic system could function without a degree of organization exceeding that which we have used in the simulation studies. Even this degree of structure, however, resulted in extremely simple stimuli.

[2] It seems evident that further understanding of machine learning requires resynthesis in operational terms of the conceptual framework provided by the Liebwald-Schurstein-Higgins suggestion that memory traces are renewed by associative stochastic increments to ideometric pathways shared by stimulus-coupled functional elements.

[3] Not only is machine learning possible, but in fact, it occurs under conditions of considerable difficulty. Indeed, it appears that even the simplest machines have a great amount of innate "curiosity" (where, by "curiosity," of course, we do not mean to imply that anthropomorphic categories or judgments should be applied to machines, but merely that the machines have a desire to learn).

James E. Miller

HOW NEWTON DISCOVERED THE LAW OF GRAVITATION

Another wasteful use of scientific manpower results from the fact that we overload productive scientists with far too many committee, study panel, and advisory commission duties, and with money raising and formal administrative activities.

—WARREN WEAVER
"A Great Age For Science," in
Goals for Americans

The investigator may be made to dwell in a garret, he may be forced to live on crusts and wear dilapidated clothes, he may be deprived of social recognition, but if he has time, he can steadfastly devote himself to research. Take away his free time and he is utterly destroyed as a contributor to knowledge.

—W. B. CANNON
in *The Way Of An Investigator*

A tremendous increase in the number of vigorous young workers in the scientific vineyard has been one of the happiest results of the recent expansion, encouraged and nourished by our Federal Government, of scientific research in this country. These neophytes, left to their own devices by harassed research directors, have often found themselves without adequate guidance through the intricacies of governmental sponsorship; but, fortunately, they can find inspiration in the story of Sir Isaac Newton, his development of the law of gravitation, and his experiences as director of the Subproject for Apples of the Fruit-Improvement Project, sponsored by His Majesty's Government of Great Britain in cooperation with a syndicate of British fruit-growers.

Few are familiar with the details of Newton's twenty-year search for a proof of his hypothesis: the frustrations and failures, the need for accurate measurements of the earth's radius and for a mathematical tool that Newton himself was forced to invent, and the integration of his scattered efforts by the splendid organization of the Fruit-Improvement Project. These details have been collected from his *Principia*, personal letters, notebooks and other papers, and a series of personal interviews arranged by a medium of the author's acquaintance.

In 1665 the young Newton became a professor of mathematics in the University of Cambridge, his alma mater. His devotion to his work and his capabilities as a teacher and friend of the student may be assumed without question. It is well to point out also that he was no dreamy, impractical inhabitant of an ivory tower. His services to his college went far beyond the mere act of classroom teaching: he was an able and active member of the college's curriculum committee, the board of the college branch of the Young Noblemen's Christian Association, the dean's grounds committee, the publications committee, the *ad hoc* committee, and numerous other committees essential to the proper administration of a college in the seventeenth century. An exhaustive compilation of Newton's work along these lines reveals that, during a five-year period, he served on 379 committees, which investigated an aggregate of 7924 problems of campus life and solved 31 of them.

Newton the genius was yet a human being; and though in energy and ability he far surpassed the great majority of his fellow men, he found himself ultimately limited in his powers. His unselfish devotion to the important work of his committees absorbed so much time that he was constrained to turn more and more of his teaching duties over to one of his students. He reasoned, quite correctly, that the substitution of a student as teacher in his place would benefit both the student and the student's students; the former because, in teaching, his own knowledge would be enhanced; and the latter because, in being taught by one near to them in age and interests, they would more eagerly grasp at the scraps of knowledge that came their way. Newton, whose stipend was small, did not spoil this idyllic arrangement by offering pay to his student

substitute: a prime example of his sense of values and his restraint. Eventually, when his substitute had proved his ability as a teacher, Newton turned all of the classroom work over to him and was thus able to channel all his tremendous powers into the administrative work of the college.

At about this time, Newton, whose mind was too active ever to let scientific problems recede from his attention, occasionally mulled over the great discoveries of Kepler on planetary motions and the hypothesis, advanced by a number of astronomers, that these motions were governed by an attraction that varied inversely as the square of the distance between planets. One evening of a crowded day in the year 1680, a committee that was scheduled to meet at eleven o'clock, no earlier time being available, was unable to muster a quorum because of the sudden death from exhaustion of one of the older committee members. Every waking moment of Newton's time was so carefully budgeted that he found himself with nothing to do until the next committee meeting at midnight. So he took a walk—a brief stroll that altered the history of the world.

It was on this excursion into the night air of Cambridge that Newton was struck by a flash of insight which set off a chain of events culminating in his announcement to the world, in 1686, of the law of gravitation.

The season was autumn. Many of the good citizens in the neighborhood of the modest Newton home had apple trees growing in their gardens, and the trees were laden with ripe fruit ready for the picking. Newton chanced to see a particularly succulent apple fall to the ground. His immediate reaction was typical of the human side of this great genius. He climbed over the garden wall, slipped the apple into his pocket, and climbed out again. As soon as he had passed well beyond that particular garden, he removed the apple from his pocket and began munching it.

Then came inspiration. Without prelude of conscious thought or logical process of reasoning, there was suddenly formed in his brain the idea that the falling of an apple and the motions of planets in their orbits may be governed by the same universal law. Before he had finished eating the apple and discarded the core, Newton had formulated his hypothesis of the universal law of gravitation. By then it was three minutes before midnight, so he hurried off to the meeting of the Committee to Combat Opium Eating Among Students Without Nobility.

In the following weeks, Newton's thoughts turned again and again to his hypothesis. Rare moments snatched between the adjournment of one committee and the call to order of another were filled with the formulation of plans for testing the hypothesis. Eventually, after several years, during which, according to evidence revealed by diligent research, he was able to spend 63 minutes and 28 seconds on his plans, Newton realized that the proof of his hypothesis would take more spare time than might become available during the rest of his life. He had to find accurate measurements of a degree of latitude on the earth's surface, and he had to invent the calculus.

Finally, he concluded that he must find some relief from his collegiate administrative burdens. He knew that it was possible to get the King's support for a worthy research project of definite aims, provided a guarantee could be made that the project would be concluded in a definite time at a cost exactly equal to the amount stipulated when the project was undertaken. Lacking experience in these matters he adopted a commendably simple approach and wrote a short letter of 22 words to King Charles, outlining his hypothesis and pointing out its far-reaching implications if it should prove to be correct. It is not known whether the King ever saw the letter, and he may not have, being overwhelmed with problems of state and plans for pending wars. There is no doubt that the letter was forwarded, through channels, to all heads of departments, their assistants, and their assistants' assistants, who might have reason to make comments or recommendations.

Eventually, Newton's letter and the bulky file of comments it had gathered on its travels reached the office of the secretary of HMPBRD/CINI/SSNBI—His Majesty's Planning Board for Research and Development, Committee for Investigation of New Ideas, Subcommittee for Suppression of Non-British Ideas. The secretary immediately recognized its importance and brought it before the subcommittee, which voted to ask Newton to testify before the Committee for Investigation of New Ideas. Some discussion of Newton's idea—as to whether it could really be called British in intent—preceded this decision, but the transcript of the discussion, filling several quarto volumes, clearly shows that no real suspicion ever fell upon him.

Newton's testimony before HMPBRD/CINI is recommended for all young scientists who may wonder how they will comport themselves when their time comes. His college considerately granted him two months' leave, without pay, while he was before the committee, and the Dean of Research sent him off with a joking admonition not to come back without a fat contract. The committee hearing was open to the public and was well attended, though it has been suggested that many of the audience had mistaken the hearing room of HMPBRD/CINI for that of HMCEVAUC—His Majesty's Committee for the Exposure of Vice Among the Upper Classes.

After Newton was sworn to tell the truth and had denied that he was a member of His Majesty's Loyal Opposition, had ever written any lewd books, had traveled in Russia, or had seduced any milkmaids, he was asked to outline his proposal. In a beautifully simple and crystal-clear, ten-minute speech, delivered extemporaneously, Newton explained Kepler's laws and his own hypothesis, suggested by the chance sight of an apple's fall. At this point, one of the committee members, an imposing fellow, a dynamic man of action, demanded to know if Newton had a means of improving the breed of apples grown in England. Newton began to explain that the apple was not an essential part of his hypothesis, but he was interrupted by a number of committee members, all speaking at once in favor of a project to improve apples. This discussion continued for several weeks, while Newton sat in characteristic dignity waiting until the committee wished to consult him. One day he arrived a few minutes late and found the door locked. He knocked circumspectly, not wishing to disturb the committee's deliberations. The door was opened by a guard who told him there was no more room and sent him away. Newton, with his logical way of reasoning, deduced that the committee did not wish to consult him further, and forthwith he returned to his college and his important committee work.

Several months later, Newton was surprised to receive a bulky package from HMPBRD/CINI. He opened the package and found it contained a variety of governmental forms, each in quintuplicate. His natural curiosity, the main attribute of the true scientist, provoked him into a careful study of the forms. After some time, he concluded that he was being invited to submit a bid for a contract for a research project on the relationship between breed, quality, and rate of fall of apples. The ultimate purpose of the project, he read, was to develop an apple that not only tasted good but also fell so gently that it was not bruised by striking the ground. Now, of course, this was not what Newton had had in mind when he had written his letter to the King. But he was a practical man and he realized that, in carrying out the proposed project, he could very well test his hypothesis as a sort of side-line or by-product. Thus, he could promote the interests of the King and do his little bit for science in the bargain.

Having made his decision, Newton began filling out the forms without further hesitation. One of the questionnaires asked how the funds allotted for the project were to be spent. Newton was somewhat taken aback to read that £12,750 6s. 3d., the surplus remaining in the horticultural development fund for the current fiscal year, had been estimated as the total cost of his project. Methodically, he put down his own stipend first, and after a moment's thought he added the item: "Other salaries, travel, supplies, and overhead: £12,750 0s. 0d."

A true believer in correct administrative procedures, Newton sent the completed forms by special messenger to the Dean of Research, for transmittal through proper channels to HMPBRD/CINI.

His adherence to established procedure was rewarded a few days later when the Dean of Research summoned him and outlined a new plan, broader in scope and more sweeping in its conception. The Dean pointed out that not only apples, but also cherries, oranges, lemons, and limes fell to the earth, and while they were about it they might as well obtain a real, man-sized government contract to cover all the varieties of fruit that grow above the ground. Newton started to explain the misunderstanding about the apples; but he stopped rather than interrupt the Dean, who was outlining a series of conferences he proposed to organize among fruit-growers and representatives of various departments of His Majesty's Government. The Dean's eyes began to glaze as he talked, and he became unaware that anybody else was in the room. Newton had an important committee meeting at that time, so he quietly went out the door, leaving the Dean of Research in an ecstasy of planning.

The seasons passed, while Newton led a busy, useful life as a member of many committees and chairman of some. One dark winter's day he was called again to the office of the Dean of Research. The Dean was beaming: he proudly explained to Newton all about the new contract he had obtained to study the relationship between breed, quality, and rate of fall of all the varieties of fruit that grow above the ground. The project was to be supported by no less than five different branches of His Majesty's Government plus a syndicate of seven large fruit-growers. Newton's part in the project was to be small but important: he was to direct the Subproject for Apples.

The following weeks were busy ones for Newton. Though relieved from his committee work (a young instructor of Greek, Latin, history, and manual training took his place on the committees), he found himself cast into a morass of administrative problems: forms to be filled out for the governmental departments, for the fruit-growers, for the Dean of Research, for the Assistant Dean of Research, and for the financial office of the college; prospective research assistants to be interviewed and hired; office and laboratory space to be wangled from other projects on the campus. The wide abilities of our great genius are fully demonstrated by the way he piloted his subproject during its first formative weeks. He personally filled out 7852 forms, often in quintuplicate and sextuplicate; he interviewed 306 milkmaids and hired 110 of them as technical assistants. With his own hands he cleaned out an abandoned dungeon in a nearby castle for use as subproject headquarters; and, turning carpenter in typically versatile fashion, he erected 12 temporary buildings to house his staff. These buildings, used today as classrooms, stand as a monument to Newton's career.

Soon the subproject was fully implemented, documented, and regimented. Newton was not quite sure what his reconverted milkmaids could do for his hypothesis (he was a lifelong bachelor and hence not well acquainted with the ways of women), but he abhorred the thought of idleness in his staff. So he divided them into six teams, each of which was to measure and tabulate the rate of fall of one variety of apple, using sufficient apples to establish a statistically significant result. All went well except with the winesap team, who discovered a new way of making applejack, and consequently ran short of apples. Newton made a note of their recipe, wisely comprehending long before his fellow scientists the advantages of serendipity, or finding good things while looking for other things.

This period of life was a happy and profitable one for Newton. From the time he arose in the morning until, exhausted with honest labor, he dropped late at night back into his humble bed of straw, he spent each day filling out payroll forms for his milkmaids, ordering pens and paper, answering the questions of the financial office, and showing distinguished visitors and the Dean of Research around his subproject. Often he discussed the past, present, and future work of his project with representatives of the five governmental departments and seven fruit-growers who had been sent to check on his progress. He was frequently invited to give progress reports in person at the central offices of these 12 sponsors. Each week he wrote out a full progress report, which was duplicated and sent by special messenger to 3388 other projects sponsored by His Majesty's Government throughout the British Isles.

One of these remarkable documents, in an excellent state of preservation, can be found in the Museum of the Horticultural Society of Western Wales, in the village of Merthyr Tydfil. In typically logical style, the report, bound in a dark red stiff cover bearing the project number, HM2wr3801-g-(293), stamped in gold leaf, opens with a succinct table of contents:

1. Administration
2. Conferences
3. Correspondence
4. Supplies
5. Results of research

The last section, "Results of research," may have been lost during the intervening years, or it may not have been specifically required under the terms of His Majesty's contracts of that era. At any rate, it is not there. But the other sections remain to gladden the hearts of those permitted to read them. Is it too much to hope that this report can be published and distributed among our young scientists in America? Such a precept should accomplish miracles for the morale and spirit of our neo-geniuses.

One day, in 1685, Newton's precise schedule was interrupted, through no fault of his own. He had set aside a

Tuesday afternoon to receive a committee of vice-presidents of the fruit-growing syndicate when, much to his horror and Britain's deep sorrow, the news spread that the whole committee had been destroyed in a three-stagecoach smashup. As once before, Newton found himself with a hiatus. He took a leisurely walk through the luscious vineyards of the subproject on Grapes, but not, of course, until he had obtained security clearance at the gate. While on this walk, there came to him, he knew not how ("Ye thought just burst upon me," he later wrote), a new and revolutionary mathematical approach which, in less time than it takes to tell about it, could be used to solve the problem of attraction in the neighborhood of a large sphere. Newton realized that the solution to this problem provided one of the most exacting tests of his hypothesis; and, furthermore, he knew, without need of pen and paper to demonstrate the fact to himself, that the solution fully supported his hypothesis. We can well imagine his elation at this brilliant discovery; but we must not overlook his essential humility, which led him forthwith to kneel and offer thanks to the King for having made the discovery possible.

On his return from this walk, Newton stopped a moment to browse in a bookstore, where he accidentally knocked a book to the floor. With apologies to the proprietor, who seemed in a mood to toss him out upon his ear, Newton retrieved the book and dusted it off. It was Norwood's *Sea-Mans Practice,* dated 1636. Opening the book at random, Newton found it contained the exact information of the length of a latitude degree that he required for the complete test of his hypothesis. Almost instantaneously, one part of his brain performed several lightning calculations and presented the result for the other part to examine; and there it was: the proof complete and irrefutable. Newton glanced at the hourglass in the shopkeeper's window and, with a start, remembered that he was due back at the dungeon to sign the milkmaids' time slips as they checked out for the day. He hurried out of the bookshop with the book under his arm, forgetting in his zeal that he had not paid for it.

Thus it was that His Majesty's Government supported and encouraged Newton during the trying years in which he was putting his hypothesis to the test. Let us not dally with the story of Newton's efforts to publish his proof, the misunderstanding with the editor of the *Horticulture Journal,* the rejections by the editors of *The Backyard Astronomer* and *Physics for the Housewife.* Suffice it to say that Newton founded his own journal in order to make sure that his proof would be published without invalidating alterations. Regrettably, he named his journal *Star and Planet,* with the result that he was branded a subversive, since Star could mean Red Star and Planet could mean Plan-It. Newton's subsequent testimony before the Subcommittee for Suppression of Non-British Ideas remains as a convincing demonstration of the great qualities that combined to make him a genius. Eventually, he was exonerated, and after enjoying many years of the fame that was due him, reigning one day each year as King of the Apple Festival, Newton died happily.

Nicholas Vanserg

MATHMANSHIP

Nicholas Vanserg, author of the following paper, is the present director in absentia of Tautological Research in the Vanserg Laboratory. Recently, he returned to his ancestral Holland for graduate training at the University of Leyden, but as he unfortunately failed to pass his examination in mathematics—a shock which he ruefully refers to as his personal Leyden Jar—his doctor's degree may be charitably designed a Dutch Treat.

In addition to articles published in Economic Geology *and the* Boston Herald, *he has had manuscripts rejected by* Time *and* The New Yorker . . . *(N.V.)*

IN an article published a few years ago, the writer (1) intimated with befitting subtlety that since most concepts of science are relatively simple (once you understand them), any ambitious scientist must, in self-preservation, prevent his colleagues from discovering that *his* ideas are simple too. So, if he can write his published contributions obscurely and uninterestingly enough, no one will attempt to read them, but all will instead genuflect in awe before such erudition.

What is Mathmanship?

Above and beyond the now-familiar recourse of writing in some language that looks like English but isn't, such as

Geologese, Biologese, or, perhaps most successful of all, Educationalese (2), is the further refinement of writing everything possible in mathematical symbols. This has but one disadvantage; namely, that some designing skunk equally proficient in this low form of cunning may be able to follow the reasoning and discover its hidden simplicity. Fortunately, however, any such nefarious design can be thwarted by a modification of the well-known art of gamemanship (3).

The object of this technique, which may, by analogy, be termed *Mathmanship,* is to place unsuspected obstacles in the way of the pursuer until he is obliged, by a series of delays and frustrations, to give up the chase and concede his mental inferiority to the author.

The Typographical Trick

One of the more rudimentary practices of mathmanship is to slip in the wrong letter, say a ν for a τ. Even placing an exponent on the wrong side of the bracket will do wonders. This subterfuge, while admittedly an infraction of the ground rules, rarely incurs a penalty, as it can always be blamed on the printer. In fact, the author need not stoop to it himself as any copyist will gladly enter into the spirit of the occasion and cooperate voluntarily. You need only be trusting and not read the proof.

Strategy of the Secret Symbol

But if, by some mischance, the equations don't get badly garbled, the mathematics is apt to be all too easy to follow, *provided* the reader knows what the letters stand for. Here then is your firm line of defense: at all cost *prevent him from finding out!*

Thus you may state in fine print in a footnote on page 35 that V^a is the total volume of a phase and then on page 873 introduce V^a out of a clear sky. This, you see, is not actually cheating because after all, or rather before all, you did tell what the symbol meant. By surreptitiously introducing one by one all the letters of the English, Greek and German alphabets right-side up and upside down, you can make the reader, when he wants to look up any topic, read the book backward in order to find out what they mean. Some of the most impressive books read about as well backward as forward anyway.

But, should reading backward become so normal as to be considered straightforward, you can always double back on the hounds. For example, introduce κ on page 66 and avoid defining κ until page 86.* This will make the whole book required reading.

The Pi-throwing Contest or Humpty-Dumpty Dodge

Although your reader may eventually catch up with you, you can throw him off the scent temporarily by making him *think* he knows what the letters mean. For example, every schoolboy knows what π stands for, so you can hold him at bay by heaving some entirely different kind of π into the equation. The poor fellow will automatically multiply by 3.1416, then begin wondering how a π got into the act anyhow, and finally discover that all the while π was osmotic pressure. If you are careful not to warn him, this one is good for a delay of about an hour and a half.

This principle, conveniently termed *pi-throwing* can, of course, be modified to apply to any other letter. Thus you can state perfectly truthfully on page 141 that F is free energy so if Gentle Reader has read another book that used F for *Helmholtz* free energy he will waste a lot of his own free energy trying to reconcile your equations before he thinks to look for the footnote tucked away at the bottom of page 50, dutifully explaining that what you are talking about all the time is *Gibbs* free energy, which he always thought was G.

* All these examples are from published literature. Readers desiring specific references may send a self-addressed stamped envelope. I collect uncanceled stamps.—N. Vanserg

Meanwhile you can compound his confusion by using *G* for something else, such as "any extensive property." *F*, however, is a particularly happy letter as it can be used not only for any unspecified brand of free energy but also for fluorine, force, friction, Faradays or a function of something or other, thus increasing the degree of randomness, *dS*. (*S*, as everyone knows stands for entropy, or maybe sulfur.) The context, of course, will make the meaning clear, especially if you can contrive to use several kinds of *F*'s or *S*'s in the same equation.

For all such switching of letters on the reader, you can cite unimpeachable authority by paraphrasing the writing of an eminent mathematician (4):

> "When I use a letter it means just what I choose it to mean—neither more nor less . . . the question is, which is to be master—that's all."

The Unconsummated Asterisk

Speaking of footnotes (I was, don't you remember?) a subtle ruse is the "unconsummated asterisk" or "ill-starred letter." You can use P^* to represent some pressure difference from P, thus tricking the innocent reader into looking at the bottom of the page for a footnote. There isn't any, of course, but by the time he has decided that P must be some registered trademark, as in the magazine advertisements, he has lost his place and has to start over again. Sometimes, just for variety, you can use, instead of an asterisk, a heavy round dot or bar over certain letters. In doing so, it is permissible to give the reader enough veiled hints to make him *think* he can figure out the system; but do not at any one place explain the general idea of this mystic notation, which must remain a closely guarded secret known only to the initiated. Do not disclose it, under pain of expulsion from the fraternity. Let the Baffled Barbarian beat his head against the wall of mystery. It may be bloodied, but if it is unbowed you lose the round.

The other side of the asterisk gambit is to use a superscript as a key to a *real* footnote. The knowledge seeker reads that S is -36.7^{14} calories and thinks, "Gee what a whale of a lot of calories," until he reads to the bottom of the page, finds footnote 14 and says, "oh."

The "Hence" Gambit

But after all, the most successful device in mathmanship is to leave out one or two pages of calculations and for them substitute the word "hence," followed by a colon. This is guaranteed to hold the reader for a couple of days figuring out how you got hither from hence. Even more effective is to use "obviously" instead of "hence," since no reader is likely to show his ignorance by seeking help in elucidating anything that is obvious. This succeeds not only in frustrating him but

* April fool. See what I mean?

also in bringing him down with an inferiority complex, one of the prime *desiderata* of the art.

These, of course, are only the most common and elementary rules. The writer has in progress a two-volume work on mathmanship, complete with examples and exercises. It will contain so many secret symbols, cryptic codes and hence-gambits that no one (but no one) will be able to read it.

REFERENCES CITED

1. VANSERG, NICHOLAS
"How to Write Geologese," *Economic Geology*. Vol. 47, (1952), pp. 220-223.

2. CARBERRY, JOSIAH
Psychoceramics. p. 1167, Brown University Press, 1945.

3. POTTER, STEPHEN
Theory and Practice of Gamesmanship or the Art of Winning Games without Actually Cheating. London: R. Hart-Davis, 1947.

4. CARROLL, LEWIS
Complete Works. p. 214, New York: Modern Library Inc.

R. Arnold Le Win

LOGARITHMIC AND ARYTHMIC EXPRESSION OF A PHYSIOLOGICAL FUNCTION

> *Like error hunting, the love of ease in intellectual matters goes with the Lilliputian outlook, whose typical handiwork is the digest. Whether of an article, a book, an opera, or a philosophy, the digest anticipates collective judgment by eliminating what is unexpected and difficult. Take out everything that anybody might object to or stumble at and you have reached your goal: the old bare bone, the one simple point, the upshot—all that is worth passing on. The word we apply, with a mystic's confidence, to this residue is "basic."*
>
> —JACQUES BARZUN
> *The House of Intellect*

1. Introduction
2. Materials and Methods
3. Results
4. Conclusions
5. Discussion
6. Summary*
7. Bibliography

1. Ben Lomond, M., Morowitz, A., Horowitz, B., and Tomorrowitz, Gon. The path of pi-mesons in an oscillating

piezo-electric field in Israel. *Pal. J. Chem. Phys., 17:* 81–88, 1954.

2. Itsu, Mitsu, Tayuhara, Isochie, Shugiwara, Hatsuyama, Miwa, and Fan Me Pink. Electron microscopy and fine structure of the limiting membrane of the flagellar mid-piece of the sperm of the gutter urchin. *Unclepsammechinus militaris. Exper. Cell Res., 4:* 18–20, 1949.

3. Jones, J. The effect of 2, 4:D, DNP, IGY, and maleic hydrazine on the growth of excised spikelet initials of "Early Glory" oats. *Botan. Gaz., 66:* 14–61, 1950.

4. Juan, Don; Smith, Phyllis; Hatsui, Irene; Fullmann, Hermione; Myschawa, Jane; Blz, Bella; Smith, Phyllis; and Oginski, Thelma. Trapstocachuamycin, a new antibiotic. *J. Biol. Chem., 67:* 1056–1066, 1951.

5. Melville, H. The path of nitrogen. XLVIII. $N^{15}{}_2$-fixation and $N^{15}H_2.OO.N^{14}H_2$ production in Chilean onions. *Arch. Biochem. Biophys., 40:* 15–18, 1956.

6. Melville, H., Washington, G., Lincoln, A., and Cadillac, de V. The path of nitrogen. CXL. Absence of demonstrable $N^{15}H_2.OO.N^{15}H_2$ production and $N^{15}{}_2$-fixation in Spanish onions. *Arch. Biochem. Biophys., 41:* 156–160, 1957.

7. Shadrach, C., Meshach, H., and Abednego, H. and C. An anaerobic heat resistant monoflagellate ornithine producing sulfur non-purple bacterium isolated from the rectum of a goat. *J. Bact., 70:* 1–11, 1944.

8. Pearlz, P., and Schwein, Alicia. A new bioassay for pseudo-iso-cobalamin B_{2a}, *Ps. pseudoisocobalaminovorans* n. sp. *J. Bact., 16:* 280–281, 1945.

9. Ramakrishnamaswami Krishnamaswaminama. Curvature

of high-frequency ultrasound waves in distilled Indian water. *Proc. Ind. Acad. Sci.,* (B) *18:* 1–243, 1951.

10. Schitz, K., and Spitz, G. Urea excretion, growth hormone production, and caudal temperature of the 6-week-old hypophysectomized, adrenalectomized, tonsillectomized castrated albino hamster. *Proc. Soc. Exp. Biol. & Med., 50:* 2–4, 1956.

11. Smith, A. K. St. G., and Smith, Esther St., G. Phenylphthalyl-thiophthalyl chloride, a new reagent for nonoses in paper chromatography. *Biochem. J., 71:* 90–93, 1944.

12. Spitz, G., and Schitz, K. Urea excretion, caudal temperature, and growth hormone production in the five-week-old hypophysectomized, adrenalectomized, tonsillectomized, castrated albino hamster. *Proc. Soc. Exp. Biol. & Med., 50:* 4–5, 1956.

13. Strickstraw, A. The fats of cats. 27. Glycero-1, 4 -alphafelitol, a new liquid component of the milk of the lion, *Felis leo. Biochem. J. 73:* 108–113, 1946.

14. Vaaraahaaha, Willi; Soderhor, G.; Torenssen, A.; and Johnson, The. Fertility, isotenicity, and agility of the sperm of the gutter urchin, *Unclepsammochinus militaris. Exp. Cell Res., 4:* 21–30, 1949.

15. Winken, W., Blinken, B., and Nodd, A. H. H. A.T.P., I.T.P., and T.V.A. *J.B.C., 69:* 12–18, 1951.

16. Wetherspoon, Jane-Mario. Acetyl-*N*-iso-hydroxbutylethanolaminly anisole esters in eels. (With statistical appendix by the Rt. Hon. Earl of Wakehampton). *Biochem. J., 71:* 94–130, 1944.

17. Zwickologg, L. K., and Arnail de la Foret, J.P.X. The effect of maleic hydrazide 2, 4:*D*, coconut milk and

gunpowder on germination, internode length, flowering, root production, and titanium uptake in the Biloxi soybean. *Botan. Gaz. 69:* 100–131, 1953.

---

* The parts 1–6 of this paper are not reproduced here because, as the author explains in his letter to the Editors:

> This paper was submitted to the *J. of Biochemical and Biophysical Choreography,* the Editors of which advised me that the illustrations were irreproducible for technical and other reasons. The Editors of the *J. Animal Misbehavior and Biophysics* suggested that the section "Materials and Methods" was unnecessary, in view of the peculiar nature of the paper. On the suggestion of the Editors of the *J. Comparative Eulogy and Biophysics,* I have omitted the "Results" which were considered inconclusive, and "Conclusions" which they felt were unjustifiable. The *J. Dynamic Penology and Biophysics* recommended deletion of the Introduction, which was circuitous and gratuitous beyond reasonable limits, and the "Discussion" which appeared incorrigible. Finally, the Editor of *Emetica and Enuretica Acta* regretted that the footnotes were unprintable, and suggested that the "Summary" be reduced to 3 per cent of the total length of text. These suggestions have been adopted.

EDITOR'S REMARKS: Since none of these references could be verified the manuscript was sent back to the author with suggestion to revise the bibliography.

Warren Weaver

REPORT OF THE SPECIAL COMMITTEE

A suggestion for simplifying a procedure, now almost traditional, by which various agencies reach decisions.

The best person to decide what research work shall be done is the man who is doing the research; the next best is the head of the department. After that you leave the field of best persons and meet increasingly worse groups. The first of these is the research director, who is probably wrong more than half of the time. Then comes a committee which is wrong most of the time. Finally, there is a committee of company vice-presidents which is wrong all the time.

—C. E. MEES

VARIOUS organizations—foundations, government agencies, research institutes, universities—from time to time face the question: Should we or should we not undertake a new or a much larger and more intensified program of activity "X?" Now X may stand for "the design and construction of a much larger, faster, and more flexible computer," or "a crash attack on cancer," or "an adequate program in oceanography," or "the building of a larger radio telescope," or "structural studies of proteins," or the production of "a higher energy linear accelerator," or "long-range studies of the genetic effects of x rays," or "boring a hole through the earth's crust," or "arctic and antarctic research," or "a large, new attack on atmospheric physics," or "an improved program for mental health," or "the conquest of space," or—well, you get the idea.

A common procedure is to set up a Special Committee of experts on X in order to find out whether X is a good idea. This committee is, characteristically, national or even international in scope, is formed of external experts of recognized standing (external as regards the agency in question, but most emphatically internal as regards X), and always contains a comforting proportion of what might be called "right names." These are men intensively interested in X, often with lifelong dedication to X, and sometimes with a recognizable fanatic

concentration of interest on X. Quite clearly, they are just the lads to ask if you want to know whether X is a good idea.

To support the work of this committee, an appropriation

is obtained, ranging from, say, $10,000 to $25,000, in the case of timid and inexperienced groups, to $200,000 to $500,000 or more, in the case of far-sighted and imaginative groups.

This money is used by the Special Committee to finance a "Feasibility Study."

Each such feasibility study results, after a period of months or even years, in a Report. This Report usually opens or closes with a short Summary Report, and also includes a long and impressive technical section, complete with charts, tables, quotations, footnotes, and so on.

This now almost standard procedure requires both time and money. It is, furthermore, embarrassingly true that those at the decision level may be impressed, but seldom are enlightened, by the long technical section, and therefore they usually have to depend largely on the Summary Report.

Having arrived at this point in describing the procedure of special committees to study the feasibility and importance of placing more emphasis on X, one is suddenly struck with an idea. Could this whole procedure not be simplified, made more prompt, more efficient, and less expensive?

Having had the unusual privilege of reading a good many such documents, I would like to suggest the possibility that, at least in many instances, these special committees, and their feasibility studies, can be eliminated entirely.

This does, of course, involve foreswearing the intellectual luxury of the long Technical Appendix. (Many years ago, the then president of the University of Virginia, Edwin A. Alderman, described a *tea* as a social event designed to give minimum pleasure to the maximum number of persons. The Technical Appendix to a report stands at the other end of the spectrum, since it gives maximum pleasure to the minimum number of persons. In certain limiting cases of what might be called a "Pure Technical Appendix," the contents give extreme pleasure, but to the author only.) The shorter procedure, which I wish to suggest, consists of utilizing a standard, universal form (presently to be available at two cents a copy in lots of ten or more) for the Summary Report.

To indicate the practicality of this procedure, I venture to suggest here a tentative draft for such a universal Summary Report. It can be adapted to a very wide variety of circumstances, simply by replacing X by a word or phrase suitable to the special case in hand.

Summary Report of Special Committee On X

1. This is a scientific field of critical importance, with obvious and widely ramified interconnection with national defense and with the health of our national economy. The intellectual and esthetic importance of deepening our knowledge in this area cannot be overemphasized.

2. This field has been meagerly supported in the past, and there is every reason to expect that modest but suitable financial support (say, roughly 20 times the present level) could lead promptly to results of the highest signficance.

3. There is ample evidence that recent scientific leads and exciting new experimental techniques are now available which combine to make the present moment a particularly fortunate and promising one for undertaking an energetic attack.

4. The long and careful study which your committee has carried out has resulted in assigning a very high priority to X. A substantial development must proceed without delay if we are to capitalize on the enthusiasm of the experts who are devoted to this field and who have developed a momentum which is a great present asset, but which might decay rapidly if encouragement is not promptly supplied.

5. Your Committee deeply deplores—indeed condemns—international rivalries in science. But we nevertheless feel

compelled to point out that the Russians appear to be, in this field X, well ahead of us.

6. Your Committee thus recommends the immediate creation of a National Institute on X (the forms will provide space here for other terminology, but it is expected that the phrase given will serve in most instances), together with a broad program of research grants, fellowships, travel grants, and so on (here again, there may be exceptional instances which will require minor changes in wording), to be carried out . . . (the form will offer an assortment of phrases here, from which the users may choose; for example, "in all suitable institutions," "throughout the waters of the oceans of this planet," "within the deep core of the earth," "in the arctic and antarctic areas," "throughout the troposphere," "in space," etc.). Your Committee estimates that roughly one hundred million dollars will be needed for initial capital facilities, including $850,000 for architects' fees, plus annual operating sums of ten to thirty million dollars (these estimates are necessarily preliminary—that is, too small).

In conclusion, it may usefully be remarked that when the Summary Report of the Special Committee is transmitted by operating officers to their governing boards, it is traditional to make some such statement as: "It will be recognized at once that the members of the Special Committee which rendered this admirable and challenging report are scientists of the highest standing, with broad and impressive experience. As the leading experts in the field X, the competence of their judgments on this topic cannot be challenged. It seems difficult indeed to see how we can afford to disregard their firm and constructive recommendations."

As a final note of caution, it should perhaps be pointed out that this procedure of concentrating attention on one single field, and utilizing the advice of those already committed to it, does have its complications. If one permits oneself to fall in love, one at a time, with a sequence of individually glamorous ladies, it is difficult to avoid multiple bigamy.

In addition to those who quite naturally consider X to be of first priority there are equally competent groups who would assign the same top priority to *A*, *B*, *C*, . . . , *Z*. If there is, in fact, a finite and limited amount of money available nationally for science, who is it that sits down on a hard chair and soberly weighs the alternatives? Is there a Special Committee for this?

S. Evershamen

THE AVERAGE WORKING HOURS OF A SCIENTIST DURING LIFETIME

Being a scientist does not disqualify a person from being an intelligent citizen.

—L. A. DuBridge

Although very elaborate calculations of the average research work-hours of a combined administration-and-research worker have been presented previously, we should like to comment on a more general case: What is the number of working days of a scientist during lifetime? The scope of this analysis is to make a good case for those research managers who refuse to grant extra week-end days to their slaves.

The average life expectation of homo sapiens in the Western World is 60 years.[1] This is actually only an approximation since (a) female scientists have a higher life expectation, since they have no wives who cause constant irritation leading to high blood pressure, cardiac infarct and other co-married diseases.[2] Moreover, their scientific life generally stops either at marriage or at 40; (b) young scientists suffer often of a very disastrous and serious, although ill defined illness: bossitis.[3]

[1] Ch. Darwin, "The Physiology of Domestic Animals," *Descent of Man,* 1871.

[2] G.B. Shaw, "Are You Crazy?" *Essays About Marriage,* 1937.

[3] E. Everybody, *J. Public Relations,* 5000 B.C., 1.1.

Barring such cases as (a) and (b), we can accept 60 years as a fairly acceptable limit.

Calculation For Lifetime

Childhood, school, high school, college, university	24	years
Sleeping—8 hours per day**	20	
Vacations, week ends, holidays (73 days a year)	12	
Unspeakable necessities, ½ hour a day***	1.25	
Feeding, 1 hour per day	2.5	
Total	59.75	years
Net working time	0.25	years = about 90 days

** Sleeping hours during scientific discussions, lectures and seminars were not taken into consideration.
*** Females more.

Summing up the above calculations, we come to the conclusion that average working days per years do not exceed 1½, and this is in good agreement with the previously published data. We have not taken into account in these calculations extra duties befalling an average scientist such as military service, or helping the spouse in her shopping.

We believe that posting of these data in a prominent place in any research administrator's office will efficiently assist him in dealing with requests of extra holidays by scientists whose mother-in-law died that day.

F.E. Warburton

THE LAB COAT AS A STATUS SYMBOL

Any distinction between the man of science and the ordinary man is no longer admissible, and no more than a form of segregation based on an inequality of knowledge. Whether we like it or not, the laboratory henceforward opens right onto the street.

—Jean Rostand
(Mr. Rostand made this statement on accepting the 1959 Kalinga Prize for his "contribution to the dissemination of scientific knowledge to the general public.")

A neat, white, knee-length coat is universally recognized as the uniform of the scientist. The lab coat's primitive function as a utilitarian garment, protective against the dermolytic and vestidemolitive hazards of the laboratory, has bit by bit been replaced by its function as a status symbol. Just as we recognize a bishop by his mitre or a burglar by his mask, we recognize a scientist by his lab coat. But in recent years the lab coat has become more than a mere work-a-day uniform. The soldier peels potatoes, cleans his rifle, and even fights his battles in his uniform; the modern scientist rarely works in his lab coat. When work is unavoidable, he will be found in his shirtsleeves, in a coarse brown smock, or in plastic. His lab coat, clean, pressed, possibly even starched, hangs safely behind the door, to be worn only when he is lecturing or greeting official visitors. Like spurs and shakos, the lab coat has been promoted to a new role; it is rapidly becoming, not merely the uniform, but indeed the *dress* uniform of the scientist.

Dress uniforms are worn solely for symbolic and ceremonial reasons, not for practical purposes. Nevertheless, their once-useful features are conscientiously preserved; an infantryman's sleeve buttons, or the spiked helmet of an uhlan, are examples. The lab coat is fraught with potentialities for such symbolic survivals. Detachable buttons were highly functional on garments subject to the vicissitudes of frequent vigorous laundering. The modern lab coat should of course be safely dry-cleaned, but the Chinese puzzles formerly used to hold the buttons in place might well be retained, and even elaborated into conspicuous ornaments—no longer detachable, of course. The utilitarian lab coat always bore stains characteristic of the work of its wearer. These could be symbolized by chevrons or flashes of suitable color: purple and red (hematoxylin and eosin) for the histologist; black and orange (sulfuric acid and bichromate) for the chemist; greenish yellow and scarlet (pus and blood) for the pathologist; blue and brown (ballpoint and coffee) for the statistician. Compact patterns of small holes or a bit of fringe on the cuff might be other symbols reminiscent of the days when lab coats were worn in the lab. Vertical as well as horizontal status could be shown by such insignia: undergraduates would wear unadorned white; graduate students might claim the right to a single, gray, grime-colored insigne; Ph.D's would wear the colors of their specialties; and Nobel prize-winners, like admirals-of-the-fleet and field marshals, would be privileged to blossom out in creations of their own tasteful design.

These developments cannot be pressed; they must evolve slowly, guided by tradition and respect for the past. But they should be taken seriously. Scientists have momentarily achieved a position of high prestige; but in a democratic society (as in any other), prestige without symbols is but fleeting, while symbols without prestige may endure forever.

*Michael B. Shimkin**

PRINCIPLES OF RESEARCH ADMINISTRATION OR ELIZA ON THE RADIOACTIVE ICE

In the fight between you and the world, back the world.

—Franz Kafka
The Great Wall of China

On the wall of many a biological research laboratory hangs a cartoon portrait of Louis Pasteur, with two somewhat bedraggled rabbits in his arms. Thirty years ago, no painting of a research scientist prominent enough for portraiture was complete without the prop of a microscope. The portrait of a contemporary research director is striking for the polished desk and a backdrop of a world map to hint at global contemplation.

Pushing unto a century ago, Claude Bernard (1) gave the world his ideas regarding the thought and action of a research scientist. Further analysis of these strange but apparently useful specimens have appeared in the literature (2, 3). Industry first discussed research as an organizational, administrative problem some thirty years ago (4). More recently one symposium (5) on the subject was chiefly concerned with budget,

* The opinions expressed in this publication are not necessarily those of any institution or individual, including the author. Wearing two hats apparently causes pinching in shoes that fit.

application forms and the desirability of sending research workers to one professional meeting per year.

Progress has caught up with research, but good. Financial support for research work is sky-rocketing. The carefully nurtured public demand for the wonders of science is steady and inexorable. Bright young men,* with a gleam in their eyes, have leaped forward to meet the need and to bring order out of research chaos. The ability to organize, sell the program and interpret the achievements to legislators and crusty trustees has become essential in research. This field, with the appurtenances of office and salary of Directors, has also aroused the acquisitive instinct of a segment of scientists, particularly those fresh out of ideas or tired of hard bench work. The battle dress of this better breed of man is of a humble Servant of Science. The battle cry is: "Science must become manageable!"

A few shortsighted individuals keep on writing that, at least for basic† research, the best organization is no organization at all, or as little of it as possible (6). Some have even suggested that personal pleasure and satisfaction are as high motives in research as are position or money (7). A pat statement has been heard to the effect that the only cardinal sins in research are orthodoxy and cynicism. The idea that research is individualistic and does not lend itself to techniques developed in industry, child psychology and mass selling apparently dies hard. But such reactionary concepts are mentioned only to be dismissed. It is admitted that administration of research is not perfect; it is a recent field and needs experience. This no doubt will be stimulated by special courses on Science Management (8). The Personal Evaluation Card (9) will do the rest.

Already there have appeared forecasts (10) on how research might be done with the full application of modern managerial practices. The utopia of research administration, however,

* Anyone five years younger, chronologically or professionally, than you are.

† Basic research is research you are doing; applied research is what the other fellow is trying to do.

cannot be reached without its price in stress and strain. A hiatus, no wider than a man's hand, has appeared between the research director and the research worker. In a spot here and there, the two are beginning to talk different languages or, even worse, to attach different meanings to the same words. That's bad; for the Director because it may hamper him in Implementing the Objective, and for the research Worker because it may make him lose sight of the Fundamental Policy.

Something has got to be done. The clock cannot be turned back. Progress must continue unhampered. A Clarification of Principles is definitely in order.

At the risk of demonstrating that "'tis a dirty bird that fouls its own nest," the author has undertaken this delicate task. Unfortunately, no Official Body has assigned him to the task, nor is he a member of the proper Committee on the subject. He therefore has neither the official status nor the benefit of combined thinking, and the results cannot be considered definitive. But, after all, *somebody* has to prepare the first draft of the agenda, and it is high time, too.

1. *The Whole Picture Principle.* It is axiomatic that research scientists are so wrapped up in their own narrow endeavors and are so unworldly that they cannot possibly see the Whole Picture of anything, including their own research. Moreover, research scientists have an unpleasant way of forcing their concepts upon their assistants. It naturally follows that really big programs of research should be guided not by research scientists but by trained administrators who grasp the Whole Picture. Pursued to its logical conclusion, the Director of research should know as little as possible about the specific subject of research he is administering. Then the forest is not lost because of the trees, and the Director really can be objective and unbiased about the whole thing.

The research Worker applies the principle in his own manner. He believes that the Director does not know what he is talking about because he has had no training in the particular subspecialty that happens to be involved. If the Director has quite a reputation in science, he still cannot be anything but a dilettante in the special field or has lost touch with the basic problem. So far as real research is concerned, therefore, Directors simply can never grasp the Whole Picture.*

2. *The Clean Canary Principle.* It is axiomatic that research scientists are a valuable commodity. The Director, therefore, must protect them carefully (including from themselves), humor their tempers and coddle them in order to maintain the highest possible production rate. Like canaries, research scientists must be kept clean and ignorant so that they will best sing their little songs. Naturally, no one tells canaries how to sing, especially not those who have never been canaries but are experts on bird seed. It follows that there must be Freedom of Science. This freedom is a delicate thing and can easily be perverted to licence. Certainly it does not extend to hiring of personnel, determining budgets or publishing papers without proper clearance.†

The research Worker also has accepted this principle. The Director must be kept clean and ignorant. He is always polite to the Director, because the Director can cut him off at his pockets, and he must always create the impression that the Director is running a Happy Ship. But tell him nothing unless it is asked, particularly about research which he does not understand anyway, until it can be written down in a self-laudatory Annual Report.

3. *The Layer Cake Principle.* It is axiomatic that Good Administrative Practices apply in research as they do to other human endeavors. Any research institution must have a Table of Organization, with squares of progressively decreasing size from the Director down, solid vertical lines connecting the squares and dotted horizontal lines to hither and yon. The alternative, of playing research by ear, with shifting and chang-

* It is probable that the Whole Picture in research is a mirror.
† Whoever heard of canaries buying their own bird seed anyway?

ing areas of activity, is most disconcerting and almost impossible to explain to legislators and trustees. Since no good administrator has more than six people report directly to him, a deep, self-reproducing stratum of administration is created. None of these layers can make policy decisions without clearance from the top, and the clerical staffs deal with all routine details.* This allows the Director to ponder on the Whole Picture.

The research Worker has accepted the principle. He seeks and competes for the higher squares, even if that elbows a few conferees on the way. Little Tables of Organization are set up in every subunit of the institution. Better positions and more resounding titles can thus be achieved. Perhaps the worker, too, can be a Director, or at least a Head of a Unit.

4. *The Combined Thinking Principle.* It is axiomatic that two heads are better than one, and a dozen is a nice, even number. Clean administrative practices require that Directors have councils, consultants and committees.† With these essential armamentoria, he can carefully count noses and arrive at safe, sound decisions that neither satisfy nor antagonize anyone. Moreover, if anything goes wrong, the responsibility can be graciously divided and erroneous decisions supported by the full minutes of the meeting. An important criterion for selection of advisory groups is that the men will Play on the Team. This is facilitated by including a majority from those who depend on the institution for some of the funds, a situation which results in mutual respect and polite exchanges of back scratching.

The research Worker bemoans the heavy expenditure of time on various subcommittees only less slightly than being left off such committees. The relative anonymity of numbers

* Policy is anything you want to decide yourself, period; routine details are anything you don't want to be bothered with.

† A mathematical formulation of this principle has been developed in a classical paper by B.S. Old "On the mathematics of committees, boards, and panels." *Scient. Monthly*, 63: 129–134, 1946.

allows guerilla raids on research workers with whom he is in disagreement. And it creates such a rich opportunity to get in good with the Director and perhaps actually to influence the administration of the institution. It is sometimes even possible, through proper memoranda, to impress the Director that the research Worker who has written the report may be a logical man to direct the effort under consideration.

5. *The Mother Hen Principle.* It is axiomatic that a hen is known by the eggs it lays and that the eggs must pass the candling test. It follows that all research performed by an institution must pass the purity standard and that the Director stands behind each egg produced. The data must be supported by adequate statistical proof. The conclusion must not ex-

trapolate beyond the facts demonstrated by the data. And beware of cogitations, theories or guesses, except when they are disguised in the discussion of the report with plenty of cross references to alternative guesses, which appeared some years before in the unreliable foreign literature. Imaginative stuff that is subsequently disproved may cast adverse criticism upon the institution or its Director. This is particularly dangerous when all important work is first released from the Director's office, thus tying him too closely to work he might want to forget at a later date.

The research Worker sees a rich opportunity to cut down some competition through the full use of this principle. The Editorial Committee becomes a bastion of defense of the honor of the Institution. Some research workers, under the circumstances, develop a sense of responsibility to such a degree that they feel they must control their fellow research workers.* For the Good of Science, of course.

6. *The Loud Trumpet Principle.* It is axiomatic that if you don't blow your own horn, no one else will bother. Advertising sells breakfast foods, and advertising also sells research. But advertising is a word devoid of glamor, and no Director would stoop to such activity unless it is called Public Relations or Information. This is a specialty unto itself, and a specialist is hired to prepare releases, research stories and informational pamphlets. There is also a wide field for intramural publicity, which is considered desirable for better morale and intelligent cooperation among the workers. Multilithed sheets with a humorous human-interest angle appear to be the vogue for the latter purpose. The important thing, of course, is that proper credit be given to the Institution and to the sources of its support in each publication, scientific or otherwise.†

Long tradition has established that the research Worker is

* In psychiatry, this is known as identification with the Director, or just a touch of megalomania.

† The crisis of publication costs of scientific periodicals can be readily resolved by charging, per line, for all acknowledgments.

modest and self-effacing. Truth is his only goal, and he hates to see his name and picture in print. The acceptance of this principle by the research Worker, therefore, is as difficult as inducing a wolf to go on a meat diet. It also stimulates scientific publications, since results can always be divided into several papers for several journals, rather than being published in one concise report. And don't forget the acknowledgments.

7. *The Ample Manure Principle.* It is axiomatic that growing things need nourishment, and research is certainly no exception. Thus research can be stimulated, widened and even initiated by fertilizing enough ground by money and all it can bring. Just spread it around loosely and widely and thickly enough, and something cannot fail to grow. Who knows, a cure for cancer or a method of getting blood out of turnips may suddenly spring from some alley into which enough fertilizer has been dumped. The idea is exciting, like a scavenger hunt. Directors with adequate funds use it widely, for, after all, research is a gamble.

The research Worker appreciates fertilizer, particularly if it is coming his way. But some would rather first develop the plants and distinguish roses from weeds, and not only use the fertilizer on roses but get rough with the weeds. The latter have a nasty way of choking off the roses in their more exuberant growth. This implies that roses can be distinguished from weeds, a dangerous concept for Directors. Suffice it to say that fertilizer piled on too thick has a way of winding up as compost in which only bacteria flourish.

The wider recognition and appreciation of the principles of research administration as tentatively outlined here, as well as the extension of additional principles through the efforts of others, will undoubtedly accelerate the dawn of a new age of scientific miracles. These miracles will be polite, tidy things, well controlled and managed, with proper credit lines neatly embroidered on their sweaters. As one of our great philosophers said (11): "We don't know where we are going or how we'll get there, but we know one thing—when we get there, we'll be there. And that's something, even if it's nothing."

REFERENCES CITED

1. Bernard, C., *Introduction a l' etude de la medicine esperimentale.* Paris: Bailliere, 1865.
2. George, H., *The Scientist in Action.* New York: Emerson Books, Inc., 1938.
3. Freedman, P., *The Principles of Scientific Research.* Washington, D.C.: Public Affairs Press, 1950.
4. Mees, C. E. K., *The Path of Science.* New York: John Wiley and Sons, Inc., 1946.
5. Bush, G. P., and Hattery, L. H. (eds), *Scientific Research: Its Administration and Organization.* Washington, D.C.: American University Press, 1950.
6. Taliafero, W. H., "Science in the Universities," *Science,* 108: 145–8, 1948.
7. Van Cleave, H. J. "The Development of a Research Interest," *Scient. Monthly,* 70: 233–241, 1950.
8. Bode, H., Mosteller, F., Tukey, J., and Winsor, G. "The Education of a Scientific Generalist," *Science,* 109, 553–558, 1949.
9. Hogan, R. H. "Productivity in Research and Development," *Science,* 112: 613–616, 1950.
10. Miller, J. R. "How Newton Discovered the Law of Gravitation," *Amer. Scientist,* 39: 134–140, 1951.
11. Perelman, S. J. *Westward, Ho!* New York: Simon and Shuster, 1947.

C. Northcote Parkinson

PARKINSON'S LAWS IN MEDICAL RESEARCH

> *When a scientist doesn't know the answer to a problem, he is ignorant. When he has a hunch as to what the result is, he is uncertain. And when he is pretty darn sure of what the result is going to be, he is in some doubt.*
>
> —LEE A. DUBRIDGE

IT appears to me, as an outside observer, that the people who apply to Foundations and Trusts, to institutions associated with the names of Rockefeller, Guggenheim, Gulbenkian and Ford, should do some preliminary research in grantsmanship. Without this, they are liable to disappointment. Knowing that the money must be given away and that the income will become taxable if not promptly allocated and spent, they imagine too often that the originator of a scheme for expenditure should be welcomed with open arms. Suppose that Dr. Tapfund has a plan for measuring the incidence of philately among the Chinese minority population of Hong Kong. He pictures himself in the offices of the Vanderfeller Trust, confronted by its higher executives Dr. Grantley, Mr. Handout, Mr. Offering and Mr. Scatterbug. They are all delighted with his research plan but question whether a million and a half dollars will suffice. They feel that five million would be justified. "Do you mean Hong Kong dollars?" asks Tapfund, his original estimate having been in that currency. "No," says Grantley, "never heard of them. I mean dollars. US." Tapfund hastens to assure him that US dollars will do just as well. Grantley signs a cheque and wishes Tapfund the best of luck. The interview is over. That is the dream.

What is the reality? Tapfund finds himself in the offices of the Bored Foundation, confronted by Dr. Knowsleigh, Mr. Nevershed and Mr. Knott. Knowsleigh says that Hong Kong is colonial territory and their charter precludes them spending a cent there. Nevershed thinks that philately is more of a social evil than an actual disease and therefore outside their terms of reference. Knott thinks the scheme politically dangerous as likely to offend Nationalist China. They agree, in chorus, that the scheme is inadmissible, unacceptable, immoral and illegal. Tapfund is thrown into the street and the janitor instructed never to admit him again. He has been deliberately wasting their time. His correspondence is sent to the DA as evidence in a charge of blackmail.

But what, you will ask, did Tapfund do wrong? Here are people with money to give away. He comes up with a plan for using some of it. Why shouldn't he? His scheme, the one instantly rejected, is no more futile than the schemes they will accept. Why did they throw him out? Simply because the scheme was *his*. It would have been brilliant if only it had been theirs. It is the essence of grantsmanship, therefore, to persuade the Foundation executives that it was *they* who suggested the research project and that you were a belated convert, agreeing reluctantly to all they had proposed. This is the basic principle of nonorigination.

I shall assume, for the present purpose, that your grant has been obtained—perhaps from government, perhaps from public charity, or more probably, shall we say, from private benefaction. Your next problem is how to overspend the money as quickly as possible so as to be justified in asking next time for more. Private benefactors have an unspoken preference for buildings as contrasted with salaries and expenses. A building, after all, can have a foundation stone or memorial tablet. All Dr. Tapfund could have permanently achieved would have been a grave and headstone in the Kowloon Cemetery—and what is the publicity value in *that*? When needing or anyway deciding upon a new building, the best plan is to have one designed as the gatehouse to an existing Hospital; a commemorative archway with the research building on one side and offices on the other, including a nice flat for yourself over the offices. Essential to be near your work. The merit in this layout is that the tablet over the archway can be worded so as to suggest (without actually stating) that the benefactor paid for the whole Hospital. The wording is better left to an expert in ambiguity; for a small fee—well, relatively small—I would write it myself. A gatehouse building is best for attracting the benefactor, and a hospital, remember, can have more gates than one. But all buildings have this drawback, that the research teams expand to fill them, and indeed overfill them, leaving the final accommodation problem worse than it was to begin with. That is one reason why all research grants imply an annual increase and why all research accommodation appears actually to contract. This may involve an optical illusion, but the observable fact is beyond question or denial. It is just one of those things.

Subject to a similar law of increase is the total number of journals recording progress in medicine and dentistry. The cause of this has long baffled the scientist, and it is with some satisfaction that I am able to reveal here, and for the first time, why this multiplication occurs. Let us suppose that the oldest and most respected journal in clinical medicine (Journal No. 1) was for many years edited by Professor A. He was a very distinguished man—so distinguished, indeed, that many here will guess the name that I am refusing to disclose. He died some years ago. Now, if A had a fault (and which of us has not?), it was in rejecting all contributions with which he did not agree; which meant, in practice, rejecting everything not actually the work of a pupil. After some years, this state of affairs became intolerable in the sight of Professor B, who agreed with A in practically nothing. If the first test of medical knowledge lies in the ability to spell diarrhoea, I doubt very much if B's version was the same as A's. Their views being so fundamentally opposed, B's papers were excluded from Journal No. 1 for some twenty-three years. At the end of that time, he was instrumental in founding Journal No. 2. This began on more liberal principles, nothing being at first rejected which did not come from a known adherent of Professor A. But B had certain standards to maintain. He believed in the free expression of views, however opposed they might be to his own, but he did insist upon their being set forth in a scholarly and systematic way. He thus found himself having to reject, again and again, the papers submitted by Professor C. Of C I must speak with caution, as he still lives in a well-deserved retirement. Although an interesting and original thinker, he is thought to be hasty in reaching conclusions and careless in presenting data. Finding his papers refused by Journals 1 and 2, he became the founder and first editor of Journal No. 3, which was open from the start to the most slipshod presentation of the vaguest ideas. You will all know the journal to which I allude. You will have noticed, however, that Journal No. 3 has a reputation of its own to uphold. Its literary standards are high. Its formulae may convey nothing and its graphs may prove the converse of the theory they are supposed to illustrate, but its grammar is above criticism. Its clinical advice may amount to murder, but its pages are never defiled with a split infinitive. It is simply because of the journal's literary reputation that the editor felt obliged to reject the papers which came from Professor D. But D—as we all know—is not the man to be denied access to the printed page. He may have hesitated for a year or two—and I believe he did—but his duty was clear and he would not shirk it. That is how we come to have Journal No. 4. But even D has to draw the line somewhere. He consistently refuses the papers submitted by Professor E on the grounds that E cannot spell. That is, strictly speaking, true. There are those who would maintain that his contributions could be rewritten in the editorial office, and so they could. But I for one feel reluctant to condemn D as narrow-minded. He does not want the idea to get around that Journal No. 4 will accept anything so long as it is typed on one side of the paper. He has the Journal's reputation to consider. On the other hand, we can scarcely blame E for starting Journal No. 5. It is the recurring cycle of events which causes the present multiplicity of Journals—over eighty, I am told, in Dentistry alone.

If medical progress were to be measured solely in terms of published work, the number of journals in existence would be a source of satisfaction and pride. It must be remembered, however, that each journal provides work for a Council, and editorial staff and Board, several editors and subeditors, numerous reviewers and writers, no doubt, of additional dialogue. The time spent in research is actually reduced by the manhours devoted to academic journalism. And if all concerned were to read each other's journals (as would seem essential, to prevent duplication), they would clearly have time for nothing else. It is interesting to reflect, finally, that the few people who do research of any significance usually keep each other informed by private correspondence. This being so, we can scarcely avoid the conclusion that actual progress must vary inversely with the number of journals published. I know of one university library which receives some 33,000 journals each year and can scarcely find the staff to get them all entered and catalogued. That is, to me, a sobering thought.

From this analysis we might conclude that everyone dedicated to research must end as an editor. This is quite untrue. The editors are merely those who have failed to become administrators. What normally happens is that the man who has made a significant contribution to knowledge is instantly offered the funds with which to broaden his attack. This happened, you will recall, to Dr. Lockstock, who had been Dr. Barrel's most brilliant associate. Who could possibly forget the paper he read before this very Association in 1938? His theory was that the painters of those modern pictures described as "abstract" are mostly color blind and, in some instances, practically imbecile. His reputation was made and the Forbenkian Foundation hastened to subsidize his further researches on a lavish scale. He was asked now to ascertain whether the composers of modern dance music for teenagers are all tone deaf (as Dr. Barrel had suggested) or merely subnormal (as Dr. Lockstock himself had surmised). Here was a big project. It meant a divided research establishment. Division A devoted to color blindness and the necessarily larger Division B to the subnormal among professed band leaders and instrumentalists. Dr. Lockstock now has to organize a research staff numbering 432, some 138 being medically or scientifically qualified, 214 technically trained and 80 whose work is merely clerical. That Dr. Lockstock can do no research himself is obvious, but what few people realize is that he cannot even direct the research of anybody else. By the time he has arranged the accommodations, health schemes, vacation roster, recreational facilities and pension rights of the technicians, all the rest of his time is needed to adjust the salaries of the rest.

It is, in fact, in salary adjustment that Dr. Lockstock has made his only recent discovery. We all know the problem. People with scientific and medical qualifications are of supposedly equal value in research work and are usually offered, initially, the same remuneration. This parity is difficult, however, to maintain for long. The medically qualified will point out, to begin with, that they are financially worse off than if they were in practice. No man, they urge, should be penalized for doing research. They demand a 20 per cent higher salary than any scientist of equal seniority. But why, ask the scientists, should they be paid less for doing the same work; and less, incidentally, than they would receive in industry? This dispute has taken most of Dr. Lockstock's time since the year 1948. Why? Because all those concerned are dedicated men; and these are the last people in the world to give in over salary differentials. And what, you will ask, is Dr. Lockstock's discovery? It is this: Medical men are more concerned with status than with money. Suppose that all his professionally qualified staff are paid, at a certain level, $8,000 a year. Two schemes are proposed to the Staff Association. Scheme A gives them all $10,000 a year as from January next. Scheme B gives the medically qualified $9,000 and the scientists $8,500. Faced with this alternative, the medical staff will unanimously choose Scheme B, preferring a smaller rise and a class distinction. And the scientists? Rather than accept Scheme B they would keep all salaries at their present level. This discovery sheds a great deal of light on the meaning of the word "dedicated."

We have now reached the point at which we can lay down *Parkinson's Law for Medical Research.* It is this: Successful research attracts the bigger grant which makes further research impossible. In accordance with this law, we mostly end as administrators. We should have ended administering, in any case, remember, had we never done any research.

Rudolf B. Schmerl

THE SCIENTIST AS SEER

> *I believe that a scientist looking at nonscientific problems is just as dumb as the next guy.*
>
> —LEE A. DUBRIDGE

A recent article in the *American Scientist*—"The Naturalistic Conception of Life" (December 1958) by Professor Kendon Smith—is yet another indication that the scientist is beginning to displace the Fourth of July orator as a prophet. Professor Smith's article is mainly an exposition and defense of naturalism, but closes with a brief consideration of the relationship between naturalism and ethics—not so much the set of beliefs and values which has composed Western ethics for some time past, but rather a new ethic which is to "emerge" out of future possession of "definitive information as to the basic human rewards" and general agreement, "among the intelligent people of that day, as to the means by which these rewards should be pursued." Scientists have been peering at the world of the future, a world peculiarly reflecting their own predilections, more and more frequently. In particular, two articles published in *The New York Times Magazine*—"Now the Space Age Opens" (October 13, 1957) by I. M. Levitt, Director of the Fels Planetarium of the Franklin Institute, and "Science Looks at Life in 2057 A.D." (December 8, 1957), excerpts from forecasts of the future made at the centennial celebration of a whisky manufacturer by outstanding scientists of varied disciplines—made it apparent that scientists are preparing to add a crystal ball to their whitecoat trade-mark. It is difficult to say whether the recent awareness in Washington of their ability to influence the political balance or their natural and unscientific enjoyment of having *all* their words of wisdom avidly listened to is the more responsible; the fact remains that destiny is once more manifest and that the scientist is her prophet.

Space of course, or rather what man will do to it, is the most belabored subject. Space is going to be conquered just as time is always being annihilated. "Already," writes Dr. Levitt, "it is possible to predict with fair certainty the probable timetable of man's conquest of space. . . . By the year 2000 A.D. man should be on his way to the moon, the planets, and the distant stars." Dr. Wernher von Braun, whose name is beginning to replace Einstein's as a household word, believes that "the intercontinental ballistic missile is actually merely a humble beginning of much greater things to come," and envisions the moon in 2057 A.D. as a fine place to spend a honeymoon, to gamble and to go prospecting—not necessarily in that order. What happens after we have turned the moon into a replica of Nevada is, of course, obvious: see what else can be Nevadaized. And, we are promised, there is much else indeed. Here at last is the limitless frontier. Man is to jump from earth to moon to other planets to other solar systems, leaving behind him his trial of honeymoons, gambling debts and tunnels.

Since, however, astronautics is not going to forge ahead of the other sciences, since the life and social sciences are running just as hard with their heads just as far down, that planet-hopping creature of the future may not be man at all. Dr. Herman J. Muller, the geneticist, has hopes for a time when "human beings" will be brought into the world "as favorably equipped by nature as possible, rather than those who simply mirror their parents' peculiarities and weaknesses"—a statement which, it is clear from his elaboration, has nothing to do either with human beings or with nature. "Where offspring now ordinarily have their hereditary material picked in a random way from two different parents"—a messy, unscientific way of doing things, even though presumably it produced Dr. Muller—"in this case the offspring would obtain his hereditary equipment entirely from one individual with whom he is as genetically identical as if he were an identical twin." There will be banks of frozen reproductive cells, foster-pregnancy will be a "widely welcomed" institution, and if you would like to be the foster parent of a physicist who can play the violin—assuming that the violin survives—just give the clerk a moment to check the files.

But you will be proud of your predictable progeny not merely because they won't reflect a single one of your peculiarities and weaknesses, but also because they will be so well-adjusted they won't know whether Hamlet is tragic or funny. Dr. John Weir, a psychologist, thinks it conceivable—and as one suspects of every scientist turned fortune teller, perhaps the wish is father of the thought—that one well-rounded day we will "be able to change emotions, man's desires and thoughts, by biochemical means, as we are now doing, in a rather gross way, with tranquilizers." Change to what? Dr. Weir does not say explicitly; but we are to learn about "the genesis of human motives, values, feelings and emotions, and the way in which our child-raising procedure influences our development"; "the important principles concerning the thinking processes, as they relate to creative imagination (which) will be worked out . . . (so) that man should be able to generate creative ideas at will"; "educational practices . . . (which) will depend much less on verbal communication and more on the other senses"; and, of course, in that day, when the organization man will be so ubiquitous no one will think of writing a book about him, "how to form groups, how to develop group goals, how to select group leaders, how to reach effective group decisions."

It is true that none of the scientists I have quoted, except Dr. von Braun, fails to qualify his prophecy. Dr. Levitt's timetable for the conquest of space bars "the unexpected—wars that could slow it down." Dr. Muller foresees his banks of frozen reproductive cells only "provided that the world does not fall prey to one of the four dangers of our times—war, dictatorship of any kind, overpopulation or fanaticism." Dr. Weir begins simply "if man survives." Science, in short, can produce the Earthly or Planetary Paradise only if we behave ourselves; but, flipping the coin, if we do, it will. And this man-like creature of the future, descended from a long line of frozen reproductive cells, able to generate creative ideas at will, knowing all about the intricacies of groups, with his rocket firmly hitched to a star, is to be the Adam of that Eden. We have just been swinging in the trees.

The intriguing thing about this collective scientific vision is that there seems to be hardly any awareness on the part of the men I have quoted that their values are as questionable as the future. Apparently we are all supposed to be agreed on what a desirable world might be, just as we are all to recognize progress when it runs over us. The scientist-prophet wastes very little time telling us *why* his vision is to materialize, taking it for granted that his interests are shared by everyone. Dr. Levitt gives two reasons for opening the space age: weather forecasting will be facilitated and perhaps we can find out if life exists elsewhere in the universe. Dr. von Braun's motivations are uncontaminated by such innocent curiosity: the new and vast scope glittering in the heavens for the old power struggle between nations, and the role that men like him will play in it, are reasons enough. "The surface of the moon has been subdivided into spheres of interest by the scientists of the major powers," he predicts for 2057 and compares our interest in outer space to seventeenth-century Britain's interest in dominating the seas. Dr. Muller wishes simultaneously to curb overpopulation and remake man in the image of current genetic values, and Dr. Weir would like everyone to be well-adjusted. It happens to be very doubtful that a well-adjusted, frozen reproductive cell, mirroring none of our eccentricities, would view the continuance of the power struggle, even on an interplanetary scale, as particularly desirable or that it would possess any wistful curiosity about nonterrestrial life, but perhaps we shall soon have a National Committee for the Co-ordination of Scientific Prophecy and this minor wrinkle will be straightened out.

In the meantime we can use this divergence in scientific perspective to ask why man is to hotfoot it into space and why he is to be molded into something a little higher than the angels. To take first things first, Dr. von Braun's reason for space travel, the promise of power, is probably the one that has the most appeal to the people who pay his salary. Governments aren't likely to climb mountains because they're there, and it is doubtful that more accurate prediction of weather or classification of Martian vegetation will become controversial election issues. What Dr. von Braun is talking about is greed, which will be as much a propellant of the space ships he envisions as whatever fuel they will burn. We have grown so accustomed to having greed called something else—*Lebensraum*, dialectical materialism, free enterprise—that the spectacle of greed masquerading as science would not be particularly startling were it not that scientists themselves are affixing the mask. Politicians and entrepreneurs have hardly ever been able to say what they mean, and few people expect them to; but scientists are renowned for their devotion to the *mot juste*, and it is always disconcerting to be disillusioned.

But greed, however disguised, is only one reason why scientists can count on sympathetic audiences whenever they talk about conquering space. If no one but empire builders were on the other side of the scientists' crystal ball, our modern prophets would not get as much space in newspapers and magazines as they do. At least three other reasons have been given to leave this planet: to solve the problem of overpopulation, to achieve a longer life expectancy for the race by having our descendants watch the death of the earth several billion years from now from a safe distance and to see if we can do it.

Space travel as a solution to overpopulation has been urged by a man named Andrew G. Haley, described in *The New Yorker* of December 29, 1956, as the "general counsel of the American Rocket Society and the world's first space lawyer." Mr. Haley, who said that "the Space Age dawned on July 29, 1955, when the White House announced that this country is preparing to launch an earth satellite," sees "no sense solving problems here on earth that may be altered, perhaps even wiped out, by future journeys through space. Our physical resources are severely limited and our population is constantly increasing. Isn't that one of the biggest problems we have, leading to poverty, war and the Lord knows what? Well, if we turn the world into a vast emigration center, as I believe we can and will, then that old problem simply disappears. I see us sending millions of adventurous pioneers out into space —opening up other planets as we once opened up the West. The universe is our oyster and we're on our way."

Mr. Haley's optimism is not shared by Dr. Levitt, who can only speculate like a science fiction writer about setting foot on anything but the moon, Mars and Mercury. It appears extremely unlikely that we shall ever be able to get out of our solar system, simply because everything else is too far away. If Mr. Haley is willing to settle for what he can get, and he has little choice, it seems that his oyster will consist of just those three heavenly bodies. Assuming that the technical problems of space flight can be solved and that the moon, Mars and Mercury can be made to sustain life—and these are still tremendous assumptions—he does not really have much room for the earth's excess population. The population of Europe alone jumped from 180 million at the beginning of the nineteenth century to 460 million at the start of World War I, and the rest of humanity hasn't exactly been practicing celibacy. Current estimates for population growth in the future make it clear that more people will be born than space ships can carry away for quite some time yet.

Then, too, how long would it be before the Martian colonists had *their* five o'clock rush hour? Or set up immigration quotas? Or refused passports to anyone suspected of less than 100 per cent Martianism? Whatever the "opening" of the American West may have accomplished, we can hardly claim that it solved overpopulation problems. The people of the most crowded part of the world, the Far East, have been steadily refused admission to America and Australia, and if the moon is going to be subdivided into spheres of interest by the scientists of the major powers, it's a fairly safe bet that *minor* powers will be rigidly restricted to visiting visas.

To shrug all this off with "well, that will be their problem," as so many progress-worshippers do, is equivalent to piling up debts for your children to pay because you love them. It makes no sense at all. We are not yet suffering directly from overpopulation in America because it is not yet overpopulated. Concern about overpopulation means concern about the plight our descendants will be in, and whether those descendants will be three or thirty generations removed from us should not alter the concern. What Mr. Haley calls a solution, then, turns out to be no more than irresponsible postponement.

Advocates of preparation to leave the earth because it has only a few more billion years to go before it becomes uninhabitable seem to have a deeper and larger view than Mr. Haley. "Space travel," writes Dr. Corliss Lamont, philosopher, author and teacher, to *The New York Times Magazine* (November 3, 1957) in response to Dr. Levitt's article, "may some day spell the difference between life and death for mankind. For ages, scientists, theologians and philosophers have predicted that eventually the sun will cool off to such an extent that life will be impossible on our planet. Such an outcome may of course not be inevitable; for science over the next million or billion years may well devise means to avoid it. But, in any case, the launching of the Soviet satellite points toward the distant possibility of man's emigrating from this earth to some other planet, inside or outside our solar system, if the need ever arises. Today, then, we can envisage the opportunity of winning immortality for the human race in the world of nature." Here, surely, is a resounding statement of the ultimate in humanitarianism.

Unfortunately Dr. Lamont's enthusiasm for racial immortality seems to have prevented him both from reading Dr. Levitt's article as carefully as it was written and from considering the matter clearly. Dr. Levitt, as already stated, is decidedly dubious about the chances of leaving our solar system. By the time the sun has cooled to the point where human life becomes impossible on earth, it won't be long—since we are talking about billions of years—before all the other planets offer something less than a warm welcome. At any rate, huddling closer to the sun as the fire dies down is a far cry from winning immortality for the human race in the world of nature. Even if we could escape from our freezing little solar system and find another sun to warm us, and then another, we would have to play the same frantic game until there were no more games to play. And that is a vision of such prolonged agony that we ought to be grateful to the stars for being as far away as they are.

Something else Dr. Lamont leaves out of account is biology. Given a million or so years to develop, life has done some pretty astonishing things, and there is no reason to think that the dominant form of life on earth a million years from now will have more resemblance to us than we do to whatever creature was our progenitor a million years ago. Dr. Lamont may not care; he may want whatever unimaginable beings that might evolve from us to evolve very much and to live very long; but if that is the case, he shouldn't talk about winning immortality for the human race. *Homo sapiens* is neither the Java ape man nor *homo supersapiens.* And there is no guarantee that evolution is all uphill. Another war, waged with the instruments scientists devise in their nonprophetic moments, and perhaps nobody will remember that it ever was.

Well then, what about hurtling off into space without bothering about starving Orientals or racial longevity, but just for the fun of it? This may be too undignified a way of putting it; basic research is customarily associated with man's unquenchable thirst for knowledge or with what Einstein called "Holy curiosity"; but it comes to much the same thing. It may not be precisely politic today to suggest that basic research should be no more a law unto itself than any other human activity, but something done just for the hell of it can result in more hell than the doer bargained for. It so happens that there *are* a number of things worth doing for their own sake, and in a general way: scientific research is one of them. Nevertheless, we have domonstrated often enough that some scientific projects are much closer to our hearts than others, with the result that physicists, chemists and engineers can choose what jobs they want, and archaeologists are lucky to get one. In other words, there is an implicit value system in our support of the sciences, easily discernible from the great variety in that support. The less application a science has to the interests of a society, the less that society supports that science. Since much preparation for space flight as we have made have already cost an enormous amount of money, it follows, once again, that this research is not being done for its own sake.

Nor should it be. There is nothing wrong with valuing some kinds of knowledge more highly than others; the question is simply which ones. Up to now, scientific experiments have generally been conducted within the framework of traditional moral values and vivisection has been practiced on animals rather than on human beings. What happened in Germany under the Nazis provides a frightening example of what can be done in the name of science; in this case, genetics. That scientists everywhere were horrified by such uses of science meant that they valued moral behavior more than knowledge indiscriminately gotten, for horror is a moral reaction. To make knowledge an end in itself (the mistake, although this secular age no longer understands it was one, of Adam and Eve) is very close to doing things for the hell of it. In some fields of science and technology we have reached the point where we cannot possibly imagine what effects further experimentation will have on humanity, although the hostility between the two strongest countries in the world does provide some clue. Scientific research, like everything else people do, is done in a human context, which means, among other things, that it is imperative to ask what we are doing and why we want to do it.

This pertains to the prophets of the genetically improved, psychologically stabilized new man as much as it does to the prophets of the space age. Drs. Muller and Weir seem quite ready to sacrifice most of what man has accomplished, however painfully, without such manipulation as they propose. Underneath their forecasts of a hygienic future, there seems to be such dissatisfaction with the human race that it amounts to misanthropy. The ordinary way of having children, which Dr. Muller would like to improve, has accounted for a fair share of remarkable men and women in the history of the race. If sterile sex and foster parentage are to be the price for increasing the percentage of geniuses, then perhaps that price is too high. The decision, at any rate, should not be made by a geneticist. It is not a scientific matter.

The emotions that Dr. Weir thinks we may some day be able to change by biochemical means, "man's desires and thoughts," have undoubtedly caused a good deal of trouble in the past, but they have also accounted for everything there is to rejoice at in history. We have not, it is true, created permanent happiness in producing Shakespeare and Bach, and perhaps great art is incompatible with the sort of well-adjusted happiness Dr. Weir seems to have in mind. Does that mean art has to go? Is only the kind of happiness sociologists and psychologists can measure to be the criterion of what man is to achieve? What value system is it that impels Dr. Weir to place so much emphasis on group goals, group leaders, group decisions? The traditional view is that man is to become master of himself without biochemical means or group decisions. It takes profound pessimism to resort to them, more perhaps than is justified. And, in this two-headed frenzy to change the world and change ourselves, we neglect to ask whether there is anything worth keeping in either.

The ethic Professor Smith expects to "emerge" in the society of the future will, he thinks, almost certainly not be "one of crude materialism"; on the contrary, "we should naturally expect the subtle, long-term social values to be especially valid in a complex social existence, and several centuries of enlightened experience give every indication that they are. It would be strange indeed if these values were anything but strengthened by a naturalistic approach to human nature and a scientific assessment of human needs." Again the emphasis is on social values and social existence, again human nature and human needs are lumped together so that they can be approached and assessed scientifically, and again one detects a terrifying readiness to stretch or slice the individual on the Procrustean bed of society and science.

The visions conjured up by scientists-seers and their followers, presented to us with reservations only about our ability to hold on until the scientists can work their magic, have long ago been made familiar to the reader of fantasies. The essence of what Drs. Muller and Weir predict is contained in Aldous Huxley's *Brave New World* (1932), and the attitudes of Dr. von Braun and Dr. Lamont toward space travel are very reminiscent of two characters in C.S. Lewis's *Out of the Silent Planet* (1938). Critiques of the misuse of science and of faith in it to solve all our problems can be indications of the extent of that misuse and the depth of that faith. If, after World War II and the dozen years of desperation following it, scientists still feel free to talk glowingly, like smiling Cassandras, of salvation through science, the fault is ours. We have asked them for inspiration as well as knowledge, and we should not be surprised that they can come up with nothing better than conquering space, freezing reproductive cells and adjusting to groups.

A NOTE ON THE CONTRIBUTORS

FRANCIS P. CHISHOLM—Is Chairman of the Department of English at Wisconsin State College, River Falls, Wisconsin. Born in 1905, Dr. Chisholm attended Cornell and Syracuse, and is a recognized authority in General Semantics and Linguistics and Behavior.

HORACE MINER—Professor of Anthropology and Sociology at the University of Michigan. Author of *Culture and Agriculture* and *Primitive City of Timbuctoo.*

J. ROBERTSON AND G. OSBORNE—Cloaked in the heavy folds of anonymity, these two professional Systems Engineers are currently employed by Burroughs Corporation and prefer to hide the light of their genius somewhere within the dark recesses of their postal system input buffer devices.

F. E. WARBURTON—A 34 year old Canadian field naturalist now working on his PhD at the McGill University. His current work on mathematical models of organic evolution also includes the thesis that if there is life on Mars, it must have something resembling a sex life.

E. B. WILSON—Born in 1879 and educated at Harvard and Yale. Professor of Vital Statistics, Harvard School of Public Health from 1922-1945. Professor Emeritus since 1945.

JOHN UPDIKE—Lives in Ipswich, Massachusetts with his wife and three children. At 31 years of age is one of the nation's outstanding novelists and short story writers. In his brief career he has already published three brilliant novels—*The Poorhouse Fair, Rabbit, Run,* and *The Centaur*—as well as two collections of short stories—*The Same Door* and *Pigeon Feathers*—and a book of poems—*The Carpentered Hen.* From 1955 to 1957 he was on the staff of *The New Yorker.*

JOHN MASTERS—Born 1914. Author and world renowned novelist. Educated at Wellington and Sandhurst. Now living in the USA at New City, Rockland County, New York. Since 1951 has published ten novels of adventure, most with an Indian setting, including *Nightrunners of Bengal* (1951), later filmed, *Bhowani Junction* (1954), *Bugles and a Tiger* (1956), and *The Venus of Konpara* (1960).

S. A. RUDIN—A 34 year old psychologist who is now teaching and doing research at Dalhousie University, Halifax, Nova Scotia, Canada. As an associate editor of *The Journal of Irreproducible Results,* he is currently screening candidates for the annual award of the Ig-nobel Prize for the most irreproducible research of last year.

R. W. PAYNE—Associate Professor and Medical Instructor at University of Oklahoma School of Medicine, Oklahoma City, Oklahoma. Born in Oklahoma in 1918.

LOUIS B. SALOMON—Associate Professor of English in the Department of English, Brooklyn College, N. Y. Born in Louisville, Kentucky in 1908.

NORMAN APPLEZWEIG—Consulting Biochemist of Norman Applezweig Associates, 131 Christopher Street, New York, N. Y. Born in New York City in 1917. Educated at New York University and Mount Sinai Hospital. Is an authority on the chemical isolation of natural products, steroids, and pharmaceutical product development.

ROBERT NATHAN—One of the nation's best loved novelists. Author of the unforgettable *One More Spring, Portrait of Jennie, The Barley Fields,* and more recently, *A Star In The Wind,* as well as *The Weans,* whose adventures are recounted in these pages.

ALAN SIMPSON—Associate Professor of History, Department of History, University of Chicago. He is an authority in English History, particularly the English civil war. Author of *Puritanism in Old and New England,* and co-editor of *The People Shall Judge.*

LESTER DEL REY—One of the most prolific of the "deans" in the fantasy and science fiction fields. For over 20 years, his novels and short stories have entertained the millions. Also writes under the pseudonym of Phillip St. John. One of his recent science fiction hair-raisers was entitled *Nerves,* published by Ballantine in 1957. Now lives with his wife, Evelyn, in River Plaza, New Jersey.

HUGH SINCLAIR—DM, MA, B.Sc, MRCP, LMSSA—Is currently Director of the Laboratory of Human Nutrition at Oxford. Fellow and lecturer in Physiology and Biochemistry, Magdalen College, Oxford, since 1937. Educated at Oxford and has taught and lectured on biochemistry and nutrition all over the globe. Holder of the US Medal of Freedom with silver palm. He is a world authority on vitamins and human nutrition.

JOEL COHEN—One of the youngest contributors, Mr. Cohen is still an undergraduate math major at Harvard. Besides his usual academic interests he has the distinction of being next year's Editor (or something equally important) of the Harvard *Crimson* and is fond of writing music and poetry and of translating books on information theory from French into English.

MO TWENTE—Currently an instructor in the Department of Psychiatry, State University of New York, Downstate Medical Center, Brooklyn, New York. Born in 1929 in India. Grew up in New York and received his MD degree from Kansas University in 1956.

NILS PETERSON—A frequent contributor of humorous essays and poetry to the science fiction and "little" magazines. He, at 29 years of age, is one of the few science fiction humorists.

LEO SZILARD—Internationally known Hungarian physicist who is now a United States citizen. He was recently awarded the Einstein Medal for "outstanding achievement in the natural sciences." Working with Fermi, he did the theoretical work on atomic fission which led to the Manhattan project. Since World War II, he has been at the forefront in the battle for international control of atomic energy, an end to the arms race, and the establishment of lasting peace. Author of the recently successful *The Voice of the Dolphins.*

CHARLES E. SIEM—A California engineer-editor who was formerly the editor of *The California Engineer,* a widely circulated and much esteemed engineering publication sent forth from Berkeley by the associated students of the University of California.

DOLTON EDWARDS—Pseudonym of W. E. Lessing of Waco, Texas, who informs us that *Meihem In Ce Klasrum* was the natural brain child of a bored Naval officer sitting out World War II at a West Coast Naval Station. "Meihem" has had an illustrious history, having previously appeared in *Astounding Science Fiction, Reader's Digest, Science World,* and *Time.*

FRANK GETLEIN—Art Editor of the *Washington Evening Star* as well as being the art critic for the *New Republic.* Born in Connecticut, educated at Holy Cross and Catholic University of America, he has written *Christianity In Art, Abraham Rattner,* and with H. C. Gardiner, *Movies, Morals and Art,* as well as *A Modern Demonology* from which "A Letter to the AMA" was taken. He lives in Connecticut with his wife and five children.

J. B. CADWALLADER-COHEN, ZYSICZK, & DONNELLY—Are the *nom de plumes,* pseudonyms, and given names of three fugitives from automated justice. Although the evidence is by no means complete, it is rumored that *The Chaostron* was actually written by two jealous typewriters and one angry adding machine. The editor is convinced that the rumor is true.

JAMES E. MILLER—Chairman of Department of Meteorology and Oceanography at New York University. He is a member of the Royal Meteorological Society and is a world authority on dynamic meteorology, climatology, and weather forecasting.

NICHOLAS VANSERG—Is actually Professor H. E. McKinstry of the Department of Geology at Harvard. Born in 1896, he was educated at MIT and Harvard, and has taught at Wisconsin, MIT and Harvard.

R. A. LEWIN—Associate Professor of Experimental Psychology, Scripps Institute of Oceanography, University of California at La Jolla, California. He is an authority in experimental physiology, microbial genetics, microbiology, plant physiology and biochemistry.

WARREN WEAVER—Director of Alfred P. Sloan Foundation, New York, N. Y. Born in Wisconsin in 1894, and educated at the University of Wisconsin from which he received his PhD in 1921. He has been a director of the Rockefeller Foundation, Chairman of the Basic Research Group, Department of Defense, trustee of the Sloan-Kettering Institute, member of National Science Foundation, and is today generally regarded as the dean of American Science. He is author of several books, including the recent *Lady Luck* and *Alice in the Tower of Babel;* also is co-author with Claude Shannon of the *Mathematical Theory of Communication.*

S. Evershamen—Is the pseudonym of Dr. S. Dickstein of Hebrew University, Israel, a pharmacologist who is a frequent contributor to Dr. A. Kohn's *Journal of Irreproducible Results.*

Michael B. Shimkin—Is Chief of the Biometry Branch of the National Cancer Institute, Department of Health, Education and Welfare, at Bethesda, Maryland. From 1955-1960 he was Scientific Editor of the *Journal of the National Cancer Institute.* He is a diplomate American Board of Internal Medicine and an authority on the biological effects of carcinogens, and on various aspects of medicine in the Soviet Union.

C. Northcote Parkinson—Born in England in 1909. Best known for *Parkinson's Law,* the remarkable discovery that in any organization the number of subordinates multiplies at a predetermined rate regardless of the amount of work that the staff actually turns out. Educated at Cambridge and University of London, he has written a total of 18 books on subjects ranging from maritime history to political economy. Included are *The Evolution of Political Thought, The Law and the Profits,* and more recently, *In-Laws and Out-Laws.*

Rudolf B. Schmerl—Lives in Ann Arbor, Michigan with his wife and a son, five, and a daughter, four. Born in Germany, moved to New Jersey at age nine. Educated at the University of Toledo, Western Reserve, and University of Michigan where he received his PhD in English in 1960. Currently, he is a research administrator at the University of Michigan. He has published articles and essays in *The New Republic, The Chicago Review, Bucknell Review* and *The Cresset,* and is interested in utopian and distopian literature.

About the Editor—Educated at the University of Kentucky, Stanford University (PhD 1952) and MIT, Dr. Baker is a 42 year old experimental psychologist currently engaged in armor training research at the U. S. Army Armor Human Research Unit (HumRRO), Fort Knox, Kentucky. He has published over 50 articles and reports in the various professional psychological journals as well as another collection of satire, *Psychology In The Wry* (Van Nostrand, 1963). He is also co-author of *The Tank Commander's Guide* (Stackpole, Military Service Division) which is now in its third edition. He lives in Louisville with his wife and five children, and is currently at work on what he believes to be the first satiric scientific novel—if not the last!